Beyond Ordinary:

6 Pillars of a fulfilled Life

Evan D. Pickett

Copyright Page

ISBN:

979-8-218-56638-8

Cover design & Illustrations by: Chloe Micheal Marketing / ChloeMichaelMarketing.com

For information about this book, please contact:
evanpickett9@gmail.com / @thelifeofevanp.

Disclaimer:
The information contained in this book is for informational purposes only. The author is not a licensed professional, and the content is based on individual experiences and research. Readers should consult a qualified professional before making any lifestyle changes.

Table of Contents

Acknowledgments

First and foremost, I want to express my deepest gratitude to everyone who supported me on my incredible journey.

To my family, thank you for your unwavering belief in me, for your patience, and for always reminding me of the importance of staying grounded while pursuing my goals. It is you who instilled in me the values of personal development, leadership, and growth. Your wisdom and guidance have had a profound influence on both my life and the message of this book. I am forever grateful for your impact on my journey. Your love and support have been my foundation throughout my life.

To my friends, I am grateful for the meaningful conversations, feedback, and insights you have shared with me. Each of you has contributed in your own way, helping me to shape my life, this book, and the ideas within it. Your encouragement kept me motivated and focused on bringing this project to life.

To my readers, thank you for taking the time to explore these pages. I hope that this book serves as a guide and inspiration on your path toward becoming the best version of yourself. Your journey is unique, and it is my greatest hope that the insights shared here help you achieve the fulfilled, purposeful life you deserve.

Finally, to anyone who has ever doubted their potential, struggled with setbacks, or felt unsure of their path, I dedicate this book to you. May it be a reminder that personal growth is a lifelong process, and every step brings you closer to your ideal self, no matter how small. Keep pushing forward, you have everything you need to succeed within you.

Preface

The journey to becoming our best selves often gets overshadowed in a world that constantly nudges us toward external validation and material success. Yet, true fulfillment isn't found in achievements alone, it's cultivated through growth, resilience, and transformation within.

Beyond Ordinary isn't just a book; it's a guide to rewriting your life narrative. With practical tools, strategies, and deeply reflective exercises, each chapter is designed to inspire meaningful change. Together, we'll explore the six pillars of a fulfilled life: Personal Development, Health and Well-Being, Relationships, Career and Purpose, Financial Stability, and Contribution. These pillars provide a framework for breaking free from the ordinary and stepping boldly into your full potential.

As you begin on this journey, remember that growth is not about perfection, it's about consistent progress. Approach each exercise with an open mind and heart and allow yourself the grace to grow at your own pace. Whether you're seeking clarity, resilience, or alignment with your highest goals, this book is your guide to living Beyond Ordinary.

Welcome to your transformation.

–E

Concepts and Methods

In this book, we will explore various concepts and methods that serve as the foundation for achieving personal fulfillment and growth. Each concept is designed to empower you with the knowledge and tools needed to embark on your journey toward becoming your ideal self.

The Growth Mindset: Central to personal development is the idea of a growth mindset. This concept, popularized by psychologist Carol Dweck, emphasizes the belief that abilities and intelligence can be developed through dedication and hard work. Embracing a growth mindset promotes resilience, encourages learning from failures, and nurtures a love for challenges. Throughout the book, we will delve into how adopting this mindset can transform your approach to obstacles and setbacks.

Holistic Health and Well-Being: True fulfillment extends beyond just mental or emotional well-being; it encompasses a holistic view of health, including physical, emotional, and social dimensions. We will examine the interconnectedness of these aspects and how nurturing them collectively can lead to a more balanced and fulfilling life. Practical strategies for maintaining physical health, emotional intelligence, and strong relationships will be highlighted. (Goleman, 1995)

The Pillars of Fulfillment: We will introduce six key pillars that serve as the framework for your personal development journey:

> Personal Development: Techniques for self-discovery, goal setting, and continuous learning.

Health and Well-Being: Practices for physical health, stress management, and emotional resilience.

Relationships: Building and maintaining healthy relationships that support your growth.

Career and Purpose: Aligning your career with your passions and values to find deeper meaning in your work.

Financial Stability: Strategies for managing finances effectively to reduce stress and promote freedom.

Contribution and Impact: Exploring ways to give back and create positive change in your community.

Practical Exercises and Reflections:

Each chapter will include practical exercises, reflective questions, and actionable steps designed to help you apply the concepts to your own life. These exercises will encourage you to dig deep, confront challenges, and celebrate progress along the way.

Challenge yourself: What bold action can you take today to step beyond the ordinary?

As you read through this book, I invite you to engage actively with the concepts presented. Take the time to reflect on your own experiences, challenge your beliefs, and embrace the journey of self-discovery. Each chapter is a stepping stone toward your ideal self, and by integrating these concepts into your life, you will unlock the potential within you.

THE JOURNEY BEYOND ORDINARY

"The journey of a thousand miles begins with one step."

-Lao Tzu

What does it mean to live beyond ordinary? It is waking up with purpose, facing challenges with courage, and knowing that every setback is a stepping stone to something greater. It is realizing that you do not have to settle for "good enough" when extraordinary is within your reach.

But here is the truth: the journey to an extraordinary life is not handed to you. It is built day by day, decision by decision, with resilience, intention, and a willingness to grow.

Studies by psychologist Angela Duckworth (2016) highlight the power of grit and perseverance in achieving long-term goals. Her findings show that individuals who embrace resilience in the face of setbacks are far more likely to achieve extraordinary outcomes.

This book is a guide to that journey, a roadmap to becoming your ideal self. Through the six pillars, we will explore how personal growth, health, relationships, purpose, financial stability, and contribution all work together to build a life that is not just full but fulfilled.

Whether you are facing your biggest challenge or striving for your next breakthrough, this is your invitation to step into your potential. This is your call to go beyond what is comfortable and ordinary, to unlock the life you were meant to live.

| TODAY | ONE WEEK | ONE MONTH | ONE YEAR |

"This journey is for everyone who has felt limited by their circumstances, past struggles, or inner doubts. You are here because, like so many of us, you want to grow beyond these barriers. This book is not about ignoring what is held you back; it is about learning how to use these experiences as fuel. Together, we'll explore how to transform setbacks into steppingstones, showing that every challenge can be a powerful foundation for your growth and fulfillment."

- E

My Journey: A Personal Testimony

Our lives can change at any time, this is a truth I have experienced firsthand. Looking back, I see that every step, every challenge, and every lesson has brought me to where I am today. When I left the Army, I was struggling physically and mentally, carrying more than just physical injuries. I was rebuilding from the ground up, finding my way through the noise of anxiety and pain. I knew the life I wanted, one filled with purpose, strength, and self-fulfillment, was within reach, but where to start? It was lessons along my journey that would require bravery, discipline, and a constant commitment to improvement.

One of the biggest challenges I have faced has been my dyslexia. In school, I was assigned a tutor to follow me around like a proverbial elephant in the room which I pretended did not exist when my peers asked who they were. I thought that relying on others would only highlight what I perceived as my weaknesses. Instead, I focused solely on my strengths, hoping they would be enough to carry me. But as I got older, I began to realize that true growth does not come from avoiding our weaknesses—it comes from facing them head-on. Only when I began working on my weaknesses did I start to grow and truly succeed. This perspective shift allowed me to see my struggles as stepping stones rather than setbacks.

This journey is anything but easy. There have been setbacks, moments of doubt, and times I have wanted to give up. But through this, I have learned the power of discipline, consistency, and delayed gratification. I have learned to put my emotions aside and do the work required of me, believing that each small step would lead to something bigger. Fulfillment, I have come to understand, is a continuous journey. It requires courage to demand more from yourself each day, even when the odds feel stacked against you.

Today, my passion is to help others find their own path to fulfillment. I want people to know that regardless of their challenges, whether they stem from learning disabilities, physical setbacks, or emotional obstacles, there is always a way forward. We all have the potential to live a life filled with meaning and purpose, and I believe wholeheartedly in each person's capacity to achieve that.

I challenge you to take those first steps, to demand more from yourself, and to pursue the life you truly deserve.

Understanding the Six Pillars of Fulfillment

Life is like a building. If the foundation is weak, the whole structure is at risk. The same goes for us; if one part of our life is falling apart, it can affect everything else. But when we strengthen key areas, we create a solid foundation that supports us through life's challenges. Think of these areas as the six pillars that hold up a fulfilling life: personal development, health and well-being, relationships, career and purpose, financial stability, and contribution and impact.

Let's begin by diving deeply into each of these pillars, but first, we need to explore what each pillar means and why they're so important to living a truly fulfilled life.

Pillar One: The Journey Begins with You: Personal Development

The first pillar, personal development, is all about growth. It is about taking responsibility for your own life, shifting your mindset, and continually striving to become the best version of yourself. We are all a work in progress, no one has it figured out, but personal development gives us the tools to move forward, even when we feel stuck.

When you focus on personal growth, you unlock your potential. You become more self-aware, understanding your strengths and weaknesses. You start setting goals that align with your values, and over time, you develop the confidence to tackle challenges head-on. Personal development is about nurturing your mind, spirit, and emotional well-being so that you can lead yourself effectively before leading others.

This is a journey that never truly ends because growth is ongoing. But as you make progress, you will notice the ripple effect in all other areas of your life, from your health to your relationships and even your career. As you build yourself up, you create a foundation that supports everything else.

Pillar Two: Health and Well-Being: Your Energy Source

The second pillar, health, and well-being are about taking care of the body that carries you through life. Think of your health as the energy source that powers your journey. Without it, everything becomes more difficult, mentally, physically, and emotionally. When we neglect our health, we cannot show up fully in our relationships or careers. We become drained and less capable of handling life's challenges.

Prioritizing your health does not mean just hitting the gym weekly. It is about nourishing your body with the right food, getting enough sleep, moving regularly, and caring for your mental health. It is about being in tune with what your body needs to function at its best.

Pillar Three: Relationships: The Heart of Fulfillment

No matter how successful we are, life feels empty without meaningful relationships. The third pillar is about nurturing the connections that bring joy and meaning to your life. Healthy relationships give us a sense of belonging and support, Whether with a partner, family, friends, or colleagues.

When you invest in your personal growth, it has a direct impact on your relationships. You become more emotionally intelligent and better able to understand and connect with the people around you. This leads to deeper, more fulfilling connections.

But relationships do not just happen. They require effort, communication, and sometimes difficult conversations. The good news is that when you are growing as a person, you will find it easier to create strong, lasting bonds with others. And in return, these relationships will support you through tough times and celebrate your successes.

Pillar Four: Career and Purpose: Finding Meaning in Your Work

The fourth pillar is all about finding purpose in what you do. Your career is not just about earning a paycheck; it is about feeling fulfilled in the work you do and knowing that it aligns with your passions and values.

Purpose is a powerful motivator. When you feel connected to the work you are doing, you are more likely to be engaged, productive, and happy. Whether you are working a traditional job, running your own business, or volunteering, finding meaning in your work fuels personal satisfaction.

But what if you do not feel fulfilled in your current role? This pillar will guide you to explore your passions and talents, helping you carve out a purposeful and rewarding path. Remember, it is never too late to realign your career with your values and goals.

Pillar Five: Financial Stability: Freedom to Focus

The fifth pillar, financial stability, might not seem as exciting as the others, but it is crucial to creating a fulfilling life. When we are stressed about money, it is hard to focus on personal growth or pursue our passions. Financial health gives us the freedom to focus on what really matters.

This pillar is about creating a solid financial foundation through smart money management, saving, budgeting, and investing. It is not just about wealth but about having control over your financial life, so you can make choices that align with your values.

When your finances are stable, you will have more peace of mind, which allows you to invest time and energy in other areas of your life. Financial freedom gives you the ability to say "yes" to opportunities that bring joy and fulfillment.

Pillar Six: Contribution and Impact: Giving Back to the World

Finally, the sixth pillar is contribution and impact, using your time, talents, and resources to make the world a better place. Whether it is through volunteer work, mentoring, or making a positive impact in your community, giving back brings a deeper sense of purpose.

When we contribute to something bigger than ourselves, we feel a sense of fulfillment that goes beyond personal success. It is about leaving a legacy and knowing that your life has made a difference. And the truth is, when you give to others, you often receive even more in return.

Your Blueprint for a Fulfilled Life

As we explore each of these pillars in detail, you will discover that they do not exist in isolation. Personal development strengthens your relationships; your health supports your career; financial stability allows you to focus on giving back. These pillars work together to create a balanced, meaningful life.

Living a fulfilled life does not happen by accident. It requires intention, effort, and the willingness to grow. But with the right tools and a sharp vision, you can create a life that not only fulfills you but also uplifts those around you.

In the pages ahead, we will dive into each of these pillars, offering practical strategies and insights to help you strengthen each area. By the end of this journey, you will have the blueprint you need to build the life you have always imagined; a truly fulfilling life.

PILLAR ONE

The Power of Personal Development

"Your vision will become clear only when you look into your heart. Who looks outside, dreams, who looks inside, awakens."

– Carl Jung

In today's fast-paced world, personal development is more relevant than ever. Many people seek ways to navigate life's challenges, find purpose, and create lasting fulfillment. Personal development is not about perfection; it is about progress. We will explore personal development as a lifelong journey, and I invite you to reflect on what it means to you. Whether it is overcoming self-doubt, developing new skills, or aligning your actions with your core values, each step brings you closer to a more fulfilled and resilient self.

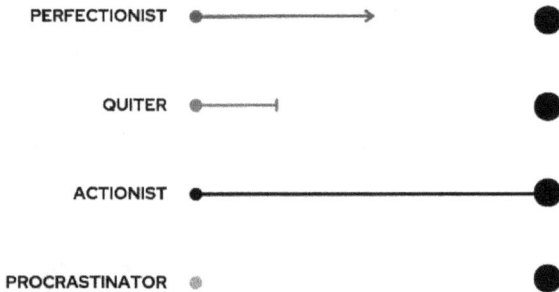

PERFECTIONIST ●————————→   ●

QUITER ●————┤   ●

ACTIONIST ●————————————————●

PROCRASTINATOR ●   ●

Reflective Question:
What would becoming your ideal self-look like, and why does this journey matter to you?

Challenge yourself: What bold action can you take today to step beyond the ordinary?

"I know what it's like to feel limited by labels. Growing up with dyslexia, my potential was defined by something beyond my control. But as I progressed in life, I realized that these limitations were only as powerful as I allowed them to be. When I decided to invest in my growth, I began rewriting the story of who I could become. I listened to myself and shifted those labels in my favor. Remember: your journey of self-development is not about proving anything to anyone else. It is about stepping beyond the limits you once thought defined you. You can reshape what you believe is possible."

- E

Understanding Personal Development

The drive to make a difference is deeply woven into the human spirit, motivating us to find ways to leave the world better than we found it. Psychologists, philosophers, and many influential figures have long studied this urge, recognizing that our need to connect, contribute, and serve gives us a unique sense of purpose and fulfillment. Research demonstrates that contributing to the welfare of others elevates our well-being, boosts our sense of purpose, and strengthens our bonds with those around us (Baumeister & Leary, 1995). When we engage in acts of giving—whether through our skills, time, resources, or kindness—we create a powerful impact on others and ourselves.

Case Study: From Burnout to Balance

Consider Laura, a mid-level manager at a tech company who struggled with burnout. Driven by ambition, she often worked late and neglected self-care, which eventually led to stress and exhaustion. Seeking change, she began setting personal development goals to elevate her work-life balance, using Maslow's hierarchy to prioritize her mental and emotional well-being. Laura gradually implemented minor changes, such as taking daily breaks and setting boundaries. Over time, she not only recovered but also saw a rise in productivity and job satisfaction, affirming that true growth begins with aligning actions to personal needs and values.

Reflective Question:
What does personal development mean to you?
How does it shape your goals and aspirations?

"Growth often requires us to confront parts of ourselves that we've labeled as weaknesses or flaws. But what if these aren't limitations? What if they are opportunities? What if a simple but purposeful change of perspective transformed self-doubt into a source of strength? Remember, the path to your ideal self doesn't start with perfection—it starts with intention and a willingness to act, accepting where you are."

- E

Self-Awareness: The Foundation of Growth

Self-awareness is the cornerstone of personal growth. It enables us to see our strengths, weaknesses, values, and aspirations clearly, allowing us to act in ways that align with who we truly are. Daniel Goleman, a pioneer in emotional intelligence, underscores self-awareness as essential for self-regulation and personal effectiveness (Goleman, 1995). The journey of self-awareness helps us understand what drives our decisions and emotions, guiding us to act with intention rather than reaction. (Goleman, 1995)

Research shows that self-aware individuals are more confident, empathetic, and adaptable. In a study conducted by Tasha Eurich (2018), people with high self-awareness demonstrated better decision-making and people skills. They build confidence in themselves and are willing to take risks. Regular self-assessment is crucial for recognizing shifts in priorities and realigning with our evolving values. This is the time to outline your ideal self and mold you into something greater. For instance, someone who values compassion might be more willing to help or practice active listening in their relationships, creating a sense of alignment between values and actions.

Case Study: Rediscovering Identity After Career Change

Mark, a former engineer who transitioned to teaching, initially struggled with self-doubt in his new role. Realizing that his value for learning and helping others had not changed, he took time for self-reflection and self-assessment. He wrote down his core values and noted how his new career aligned with his desire to impact lives positively. This exercise reaffirmed his sense of purpose, making his transition not only smoother but also deeply fulfilling.

Exercise: Personal Inventory

Strengths and Weaknesses Assessment: Write down your top five strengths and five areas where you feel there is room for improvement.

Values Exploration: List your core values (e.g., honesty, compassion, courage, growth). Reflect on why each one is significant to you.

Identify Key Goals: Consider what you want to achieve in the next one to five years. Write down three specific, measurable goals that align with your values and strengths. When we write our goals down, we bring them into the tangible world. Making them no longer ideas but actionable goals.

Reflective Question:
What personal qualities do you value most, and how do they shape your daily actions and decisions?

Challenge yourself: What bold action can you take today to step beyond the ordinary

---

DO YOU NEED...

MORE TIME

OR

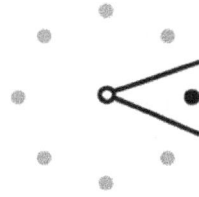

BETTER FOCUS

Goal Setting: Building a Path Forward

Goal setting transforms our desires into achievable milestones, providing direction and structure to personal growth and the journey. Edwin Locke and Gary Latham's (2002) goal-setting theory asserts that setting specific, challenging goals results in higher performance, providing a clear path forward. For example, a vague goal like "improving my health" becomes actionable with specifics: "I will exercise for 30 minutes three times a week." Get detailed into what you want out of life.

Goal setting becomes especially achievable when approached with the SMART framework (Specific, Measurable, Achievable, Relevant, and Time-bound). We have all heard of SMART goals, but have you tried implementing this strategy on one of your goals? By applying this approach, we can break down larger ambitions into smaller, manageable steps that feel attainable and encourage steady progress.

Practical SMART Goal Example:

Specific: I will exercise for 30 minutes, 5 days a week.

Measurable: Track workouts using a fitness app.

Achievable: Start with moderate exercises like walking or yoga.

Relevant: Prioritizing health aligns with my personal goals.

Time-bound: Achieve this routine consistently for the next 30 days.

Case Study: Achieving Financial Freedom with SMART Goals

Consider Sarah, who aimed to elevate her financial stability. She set a SMART goal to save $200 a month for a year to build an emergency fund. By tracking her progress monthly, she stayed motivated and even looked for additional ways to save. By the year's end, she had saved more than she had expected and felt empowered to tackle larger financial goals. SMART goal setting allowed Sarah to measure progress and see tangible results.

Exercise: Setting Your Own SMART Goal

Choose an Area for Improvement: Identify an area, like physical health, career, or emotional well-being.

Apply the SMART Criteria: For example, if focusing on health, your goal could be, "I will do a 45-minute workout daily for the next 30 days."

<u>Reflect Weekly:</u> Check in each week to assess your progress and adjust, as necessary. This reflective loop keeps you engaged and motivated. Taking small steps builds momentum.

<u>Reframe Setbacks as Lessons:</u> When setbacks arise, ask yourself, "What can I learn from this experience?" Spin it into something positive.

<u>Build a Support System</u>: Surrounding yourself with supportive people provides encouragement and strength during challenging times (Seligman, 2011). The 6 Pillars are designed to build a foundation, mastering these provides us with the tools to achieve anything.

IMPOSSIBLE?

BREAK IT DOWN!

Reflective Question:
What specific goal, if achieved, would bring you closer to the life you envision?

Developing Emotional Intelligence (Goleman, 1995)

Emotional intelligence (EI) is the capacity to constructively understand, manage, and express emotions. According to Goleman, EI is fundamental to creating healthy connections, as it promotes empathy and enhances interpersonal communication (Goleman, 1995). (Goleman, 1995)

Building emotional intelligence involves self-awareness, empathy, and active listening. Try actively listening during your next conversation, ask questions, and be interested. All the research supports the idea that emotionally intelligent people often experience better relationship satisfaction and lower stress (Mayer, Salovey, & Caruso, 2008). Techniques like active listening, focusing on the speaker's words and emotions build intelligence and enhance empathy and understanding. (Goleman, 1995)

Case Study: Feeling Heard Using Active Listening

My good friend M who I am personally working with to construct his own six pillars recently shared an experience with me where he had an opportunity to meet with a successful music producer for lunch. Ironically, the lunch was centered around personal development and M was hoping to absorb as much knowledge from this high performer as possible. M said the most significant thing he noticed about the interaction was the way this extraordinarily successful individual zeroed in his focus on what someone who was just beginning his journey had to say. He listened intently and asked so many questions that M barely got a chance to pick the brain of this extraordinarily successful individual. Instead, he was having his brain picked by someone who was using active listening. He acted genuinely interested and made M feel important despite the fact he felt he had nothing to offer before the engagement.

Reflective Question:
What past challenges have made you stronger, and how can they serve as stepping stones for your future growth?

Challenge yourself: What bold action can you take today to step beyond the ordinary?

Developing Emotional Intelligence: (Goleman, 1995)

<u>Practice Active Listening</u>: Focus on truly hearing others without planning a response. Ask questions and be curious.

<u>Identify Emotional Triggers</u>: Recognize situations that evoke your emotions and develop strategies to manage these emotions. If something is triggering, remain present and practice. That is growth.

<u>Reflect on Emotional Responses</u>: After emotional exchanges, reflect on your reaction and consider how to manage similar situations in the future. Create a positive outcome in your head, training yourself consciously and developing strategies.

Reflective Question:
How can becoming more emotionally aware
elevate your relationships and interactions?

Embracing a Growth Mindset

Carol Dweck's research on growth mindset reveals that believing in the ability to improve through effort not only enhances learning but also drives sustained personal growth (Dweck, 2006).

A growth mindset is a belief that abilities and intelligence can be developed through effort, learning, and persistence, which is a transformative aspect of personal development. Rooted in the research of psychologist Carol Dweck, this mindset stands in contrast to a fixed mindset, where individuals believe their qualities are innate and unchangeable. Dweck's research reveals that those who adopt a growth mindset are more resilient, adaptable, and open to new experiences, viewing challenges and setbacks as opportunities to gain experience rather than as threats to their self-worth (Dweck, 2006). Our mind shapes our reality, and gaining control of our mind is coming one step closer to our ideal self.

Seeing Challenges

A growth mindset shifts our perception of challenges. Instead of avoiding difficult tasks, people with this mindset see them as exciting opportunities for growth. We must embrace the discomfort that comes with learning because we know it is necessary for improvement. This

28

shift is empowering; it encourages us to engage fully with tasks, even when they seem daunting, and to persist through difficulties. Viewing challenges as valuable experiences helps us stay motivated, as each challenge overcome represents progress rather than failure.

Mistakes as Building Blocks for Growth

Reframe Negative Thoughts: When facing a challenge or setback, practice reframing your thoughts. Instead of thinking, "I'm not good at this," try saying, "I'm still learning, and I can elevate with practice." This shift in language reinforces the belief that abilities can grow.

Set Learning-Oriented Goals: Instead of focusing solely on outcomes, set goals centered around learning and progress. For example, rather than aiming to "be the best at work," aim to "learn one new skill or technique each week." This approach places value on the learning journey rather than just the result.

Celebrate Small Wins: Acknowledging and celebrating small achievements reinforces the idea that progress is happening, even if it is gradual. Speak and celebrate successes. This practice keeps us motivated and reminds us of the growth process.

Reflect on Learning Experiences: After completing a challenging task or experiencing a setback, take a moment to reflect. Ask yourself, "What did I learn from this?" and "How will this experience help me next time?" Reflection helps consolidate lessons learned and prepares you for future challenges.

Focus on Progress Over Perfection: Celebrate small victories rather than aiming for flawlessness.

Challenge Negative Thoughts: Reframe limiting thoughts as opportunities to gain experience.

Seek Constructive Feedback: Use input from others to expand your skills and understanding.

Reflective Question:
What steps can you take to view challenges as opportunities for growth?

Challenge yourself: What bold action can you take today to step beyond the ordinary?

Integrating Personal Development into Daily Life

Sustainable personal growth comes from small, consistent actions. James Clear's concept of atomic habits emphasizes that minor improvements practiced daily lead to remarkable results over time (Clear, 2018).

Neuroscientist Charles Duhigg, author of "The Power of Habit", explains how habits are formed through the habit loop of cue, routine, and reward. Understanding this loop can help break negative cycles and build empowering routines (Duhigg, 2012).

Daily Practices for Personal Growth:

Morning Reflection: Spend five minutes each morning setting goals aligned with your values.

End-of-Day Gratitude: Reflect on three things you are grateful for each evening.

Weekly Progress Review: Set aside time each week to assess progress, acknowledge achievements, and adjust goals as needed.

Reflective Questions:
How can you incorporate small daily actions that align with your values and aspirations?

Reflective Questions:

- What does personal development mean to you personally?
- How can daily actions align you with your core values?
- What goal, if achieved, would signify real progress on your journey to self-fulfillment?

Personal development is a lifelong journey. Each step brings you closer to a life of purpose, resilience, and joy. Committing to this path empowers you to become Beyond Ordinary, enriching every area of your life. This is an exciting time, be bold and believe in yourself.

Barbara Fredrickson's (2001) broaden-and-build theory shows that cultivating positive emotions, such as joy and hope, enhances resilience by broadening cognitive and behavioral resources, allowing individuals to navigate challenges effectively.

PILLAR TWO

The Power of Health and Well-Being

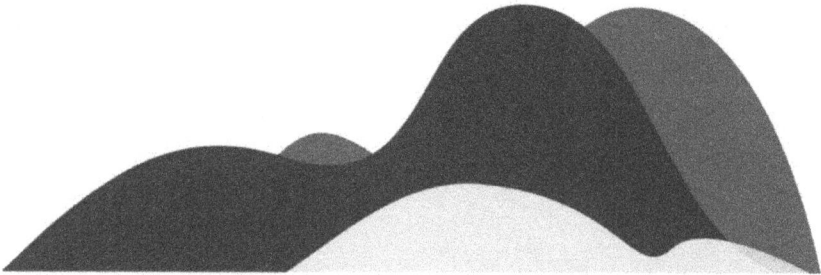

"Take care of your body. It is the only place you have to live."

— Jim Rohn

In our pursuit of fulfillment, health and well-being emerge as one of the most crucial pillars. Without a sturdy foundation of physical, mental, and emotional wellness, the path to becoming our ideal selves is obstructed. Health is not just the absence of illness; it is about achieving a state of vitality that propels us forward. Whether we are aiming for professional success, nurturing meaningful relationships, or striving to impact our communities, prioritizing our health enables us to perform at our best and live with greater energy, clarity, and purpose (World Health Organization, 2020).

Reflective Question:
How would prioritizing your health and well-being impact your journey toward fulfillment?

Challenge yourself: What bold action can you take today to step beyond the ordinary?

The Mind-Body Connection: Harmonizing for Growth

The connection between our minds and bodies is essential, influencing every aspect of our health, resilience, and overall well-being. When we neglect one area, it can lead to imbalances that impact the other, often resulting in decreased health and imbalance. But when we nurture both our minds and bodies, we experience improved health, greater resilience, and a richer quality of life. Research strongly supports this interconnectedness: a healthy mind supports a healthy body, and a healthy body supports a thriving mind.

Balanced Health: The Biopsychosocial Model

Today's understanding of health is based on more than just physical wellness; it includes our mental, social, and emotional well-being. Research shows that our minds and bodies are deeply linked, where disruptions in one can directly impact the other. For example, high stress (a mental factor) can weaken the immune system, making us more vulnerable to physical or mental illness.

Physical Health and Mental Clarity

Similarly, when we take care of our bodies through activities like exercise, restful sleep, and a balanced diet, our mental clarity and emotional well-being benefit. Physical activity, for example, reduces symptoms of stress, anxiety, and depression by naturally increasing feel-good hormones like endorphins. Regular exercise has even been linked to elevated mood and overall health, helping to reduce "mental fog" and support a positive mindset (Chekroud et al., 2018).

CONTROL YOUR MIND   OR IT CONTROLS...

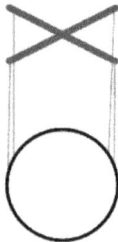

Physical Well-Being: Building a Strong Foundation for the Mind

The Natural Mood Booster

Regular exercise does not just build physical strength, it also has powerful mental benefits, one being confidence. Physical activity triggers the release of endorphins and serotonin, which can ease stress and elevate our mood. Studies show that people who exercise regularly have fewer "bad mental health days," highlighting just how much of a boost exercise and movement can bring to our daily outlook (Chekroud et al., 2018). Feeling stressed? Try going for a walk.

The Role of Nutrition

The food we eat directly impacts how we feel mentally and emotionally. A diet rich in omega-3s, B vitamins, and antioxidants supports brain health, while processed and high-sugar foods are linked to increased risks of depression and fatigue. A Mediterranean-style diet, which includes fruits, vegetables, whole grains, and lean proteins, has been associated with elevated mood and mental clarity, helping us feel balanced and energized (Jacka et al., 2014). Switching from a bad diet can jump-start your health, creating momentum for change.

The Power of Quality Sleep

Sleep is essential for both mental clarity and emotional stability. During sleep, our brains undergo essential restorative processes; consolidating memories, regulating mood, and clearing out toxins that build up during the day. Adults who get 7–9 hours of restful sleep report higher levels of focus, energy, and physical well-being (National Sleep Foundation). Establishing a sleep routine can be a simple yet powerful way to support both body and mind. Creating good sleeping habits fuels us for the day. Taking care of our minds also has powerful effects on our physical health.

Reducing Stress for a Healthier Body

Effectively managing stress protects us from its physical side effects. When we are chronically stressed, our immune systems are weakened, inflammation increases, and our risk of heart disease rises. This is why we are feeling stressed, anxious, or even depressed. Stress-management practices such as mindfulness meditation, exercise, or talking with a friend or therapist can elevate immune responses, reduce inflammation, and even help us recover faster from illness.

The Positive Impact of Mindset on Health

Adopting a positive outlook on life has had real benefits for my physical health. People who experience more positive emotions report healthier hearts, stronger immune systems, and faster recovery from illnesses. This link between positivity and physical health is partly because of reduced stress hormones, which protect our bodies from the damage that chronic stress can cause. Many YouTube videos, books, and podcasts dive into great detail about a positive mindset and its benefits.

Building Resilience

Emotional resilience is the ability to manage and adapt to challenges, which affects both mental and physical health. When you are more resilient, reports show lower levels of pain, even with chronic conditions, and tend to recover from injuries or surgery more effectively. Emotional resilience allows us to stay committed to self-care, especially when times are tough, which keeps us moving toward our health goals.

Ann Masten's work on resilience highlights the concept of "ordinary magic," emphasizing that resilience is not a rare trait but a common ability that can be nurtured through supportive relationships, positive environments, and adaptive systems. Her findings demonstrate that individuals who develop resilience through these external and internal supports are better equipped to overcome setbacks and achieve long-term success (Masten, 2001).

Practical Tips for a Healthy Mind-Body Connection

Mindfulness and Meditation

Mindfulness helps us bridge the mind and body by promoting relaxation, awareness, and emotional balance. Research shows that mindfulness can help reduce symptoms of stress, anxiety, and even physical pain. Try setting aside a few minutes each day for mindfulness practice to notice a positive shift in your mood and energy. It should not be easy at first. When learning something new, you are growing, and there will be growing pains. I promise being mindful will become easier over time.

Regular Physical Activity

Daily movement is one of the most effective ways to elevate your mental and physical well-being. Many of us have been couped up and overstimulated with sedentary lifestyles leading to stiff bodies and chronic pain. Aim for about 150 minutes of moderate exercise per week. Activities like weightlifting, walking, yoga, and dancing do not just keep you physically fit—they boost your mood and mental clarity, helping you feel centered and strong.

Balanced Nutrition for Brain and Body Health

Eating a balanced diet with plenty of fruits, vegetables, whole grains, and healthy fats helps fuel both body and mind. Stay away from frozen and processed foods. This kind of nutrition supports the brain's cognitive processes, keeps your energy stable, avoids that afternoon crash, and helps manage stress.

Sleep Hygiene

Good sleep is essential for maintaining mental clarity, emotional stability, and physical energy. Try to establish a consistent sleep routine, minimize screen time before bed, and avoid eating and drinking before bed for better rest. The benefits of restful sleep extend to your mood, your focus, and your overall health.

FOCUS   IS   ABOUT   ELIMINATING   DISTRACTION

Case Study: Overcoming Burnout through the Mind-Body Connection

Emma, a successful marketing executive, faced constant fatigue and burnout. Despite achieving career milestones, she felt disconnected from her personal life and often anxious. Emma's turning point came when she began incorporating mindfulness practices like meditation, balanced nutrition, and regular exercise. This combined focus on her mind and body reduced her stress levels, elevated her energy, and gave her a renewed sense of purpose, allowing her to perform extraordinary at work and connect more meaningfully with loved ones. Emma's journey exemplifies the power of nurturing both mind and body to promote true well-being.

Reflective Question:
What small adjustments can you make today to better nurture the connection between your mind and body?

Physical Health: The Foundation of Well-Being

Physical health is the cornerstone upon which all other aspects of well-being are built. Regular exercise, balanced nutrition, and sufficient sleep are essential practices that support physical and mental health (Centers for Disease Control and Prevention, 2021). These practices equip us to manage life's challenges with vitality, protect our immune systems, and support longevity.

"Physical and mental resilience are born from our willingness to keep going, especially when things are hard. I have struggled with my weight throughout my life, but when I took control of my body, I felt better, stronger, and capable. Health is not just about fitness; it is about building a foundation that can carry you through life's challenges. It is about discovering your inner strength and knowing that even small steps forward can lead to lasting change. If you've ever felt held back by limitations, know that this journey is yours to shape, one intentional choice at a time."

-E

Key Components of Physical Health

Exercise: Physical activity not only boosts mood but also reduces stress, increases productivity, and enhances cognitive function (Ratey & Loehr, 2011).

Nutrition: The food we consume fuels both body and mind. Nutrient-rich diets contribute to mental clarity, energy, and resilience (Harvard T.H. Chan School of Public Health, 2021).

<u>Sleep</u>: Quality sleep is essential for mental and physical recovery, promoting cognitive function, emotional resilience, and physical health (Walker, 2017).

Case Study: Achieving Holistic Health through Physical Fitness

Consider Tom, a software engineer who initially struggled with back pain and low energy due to a sedentary lifestyle. Tom committed to a new physical fitness routine, including strength training, cardio, and elevated sleep habits. Within a few months, he experienced a transformation—not only did his physical health elevate, but he also felt more mentally alert, creative, and emotionally balanced. His focus at work increased, and he found more joy in his personal life, underscoring that physical health is vital to our holistic well-being.

Neuroscientist Charles Duhigg, author of "The Power of Habit", explains how habits are formed through the habit loop of cue, routine, and reward. Understanding this loop can help break negative cycles and build empowering routines (Duhigg, 2012).

Reflective Question:
How would prioritizing physical health in your routine impact your overall sense of well-being?

Challenge yourself: What bold action can you take today to step beyond the ordinary?

When I committed to exercising regularly, I not only trained my body but also cultivated a more resilient mind and spirit. This practice does not require perfection or extreme dedication but rather a steady approach that becomes part of your daily rhythm. Setting a route and prioritizing my health. When you embrace physical health, you are investing in a more vibrant, fulfilled life. Below, we will dive deeper into the transformative benefits of physical exercise and how you can make it a foundational part of your journey.

-E

Key Benefits of Physical Exercise

Studies also show that regular strength training plays a role in managing weight and boosting metabolism. As you build muscle, your body becomes more efficient at burning calories, even at rest. Beyond weight management, this metabolic boost promotes a healthier life and can contribute to greater longevity (Peterson et al., 2011).

Picture yourself a decade from now, strong, and capable, thanks to the investment you made in your strength today. Regular strength training can become your ally in sustaining an active, independent life.

Start small if strength training is new to you. Try adding 30-45 minutes of exercise two to three times a week, and gradually build up as you feel stronger. Notice how your body responds and celebrate small milestones, like lifting a bit more weight or completing an extra set.

-E

Improving Cardiovascular Health

Cardiovascular exercise is one of the most effective ways to strengthen your heart and lungs, reducing your risk of heart disease. When you engage in activities that elevate your heart rate, whether it is brisk walking, jogging, cycling, swimming, or dancing, you are enhancing the efficiency of your cardiovascular system (Erickson et al., 2011). The key is to keep moving. The benefits extend beyond physical health, as increased blood flow to the brain elevates cognitive function, memory, and concentration.

Imagine your body as a well-tuned machine. Cardiovascular exercise keeps the engine and the heart working smoothly. Each time you go for a walk, run, or engage in a favorite cardio activity, you are nurturing your brain and body. This type of exercise is particularly effective at keeping you sharp as you age, supporting both physical and mental performance. If you have not noticed, everything is connected.

Personal Action Step: Aim for 10-15 minutes of cardio activity every day. Start with whatever feels accessible, even if it is a brisk 10-minute walk that you gradually increase over time. As you elevate, find ways to make cardio fun and engaging, dance, hike, or swim. Choosing activities that you enjoy becomes a consistent habit.

Supporting Mental Health and Emotional Balance

The impact of exercise on mental health is profound. Physical activity triggers the release of endorphins, known as the "feel-good" hormones, which act as natural mood lifters. Regular exercise reduces symptoms of anxiety and depression, helps manage stress, and can be a key tool in building emotional resilience (Blumenthal et al., 1999). Studies have shown that people who engage in moderate exercise experience significant improvements in mood, self-esteem, and even the quality of their sleep (Kredlow et al., 2015).

Think of exercise as a form of mental hygiene, like brushing your teeth. When you move your body, you are also "cleaning up" your mind, clearing away stress and restoring emotional balance. Especially important during challenging times when you might feel overwhelmed or anxious. Exercise can provide an emotional release, helping you face the world with a calmer, more balanced outlook.

Types of Exercise for a Balanced, Resilient Life

Strength Training: Supports muscle and bone health, fortifies the body against injury, and enhances daily performance. Creates confidence, delayed gratification, and discipline.

Cardiovascular Exercise: Strengthens the heart and lungs, elevates brain function, and boosts endurance. Making you able to breathe extraordinarily and move longer.

Flexibility: Improves your range of motion, reducing the risk of injuries and supporting joint health. Incorporate stretching or yoga a few times a week.

Personal Action Step: Incorporate at least 20 minutes of physical activity into your day to promote emotional stability. It could be a hike in nature, a quick workout, or even yoga. 20 minutes of physical activity and 15 minutes of cardiovascular exercise with put you in the 45-minute workout window. Pay attention to how you feel afterward and recognize the shift in your mind and body to a more positive mindset and greater resilience.

Making Exercise a Habit

Making exercise a habit is about finding joy in movement and integrating it seamlessly into your daily routine. Start with small, manageable goals and focus on consistency over intensity. Aim for movement that suits your lifestyle, schedule, and preferences. Some days, it might be a gentle walk, while others could include more intense workouts. The key is to keep moving and recognize that each step forward is a step toward a healthier, more resilient you.

Reflective Exercise: The Role of Exercise in Your Life

Take a few moments to reflect on your current relationship with physical activity.

Ask yourself:

- How does exercise currently fit into my life, and how does it make me feel?
- What benefits would I like to gain from regular movement, physical, mental, or emotional?
- What minor changes could I make to create a consistent exercise routine?

Holistic Nutrition: Maximizing Health with Balanced Choices

Holistic nutrition views food as a source of both physical and mental wellness. A diet rich in diverse, nutrient-dense foods supports mental clarity, physical energy, and long-term vitality. The research underscores the role of quality animal proteins and fats as essential components of a balanced diet, as they support muscle maintenance, mental health, and immune function (Wolfe, 2006; Simopoulos, 1999).

Benefits of Nutrient-Dense, Meat-Based Nutrition

High-Quality Protein for Muscle Maintenance:

Animal-based proteins provide complete amino acid profiles essential for tissue repair and muscle health, aiding weight management and muscle preservation (Wolfe, 2006).

Brain and Heart Support with Essential Fatty Acids:

Omega-3 fatty acids from sources like fish promote cardiovascular health and cognitive performance (Simopoulos, 1999). These fats reduce inflammation and enhance neurological function.

<u>Vitamin-Rich Meats for Immunity</u>:

Organ meats like liver offer prominent levels of essential nutrients, including vitamin A and B12, that support immunity and energy production (Cordain, 2011).

Case Study: Transforming Health with Nutrient-Dense Foods

Linda, who often felt fatigued and unfocused, shifted her diet to incorporate more nutrient-dense animal proteins, fresh vegetables, and whole foods. Within weeks, she noticed improved mental clarity, energy levels, and immune resilience. Her experience shows how a balanced diet fuels both body and mind, supporting the journey toward holistic health.

Martin Seligman's research on learned optimism shows that individuals who adopt an optimistic explanatory style, seeing setbacks as temporary and specific, are more likely to persevere and achieve their goals, even in challenging circumstances.

Reflective Question:
What foods help you feel energized and focused, and how can you make them a regular part of your diet?

Challenge yourself: What bold action can you take today to step beyond the ordinary?

Mental and Emotional Well-Being: The Compass for Success

While physical health forms a solid foundation, mental and emotional well-being serve as a compass that guides us toward a life of fulfillment. Building resilience, emotional intelligence, and stress management skills advances the mental and emotional stability needed to thrive in personal and professional spaces (Goleman, 2006).

Martin Seligman's work on *learned optimism* reveals that adopting positive explanatory styles for setbacks, viewing challenges as temporary and specific rather than permanent and global—enhances resilience and achievement. This approach has been applied effectively in educational and workplace settings to boost long-term success (Seligman, 1990).

Key Aspects of Mental and Emotional Health

Emotional Intelligence: Emotional intelligence allows us to navigate complex relationships with empathy and self-awareness, enhancing both personal and professional success (Goleman, 2006). (Goleman, 1995)

Resilience: Resilience keeps us focused on growth and helps us navigate setbacks without feeling overwhelmed (American Psychological Association, 2022).

Stress Management: Practices like mindfulness, hobbies, and relaxation techniques mitigate stress, preventing burnout and helping maintain focus (Kabat-Zinn, 2015).

Case Study: Managing Stress through Mindfulness and Emotional Intelligence

Rebecca, a teacher, often felt overwhelmed by her workload and struggled to manage stress. After practicing mindfulness and enhancing her emotional intelligence, she became more resilient and empathetic, which elevated both her personal and professional relationships. Her experience demonstrates how mindfulness and emotional intelligence provide tools for managing stress and promoting emotional stability. (Goleman, 1995)

Reflective Question:
What practices help you maintain emotional balance, and how can you make them a part of your routine?

Spiritual Health: Connecting with Your Inner Purpose

Spiritual health encompasses finding meaning, purpose, and a sense of belonging. Spiritual practices, like mindfulness, gratitude, and nature connection, enhance mental clarity, emotional stability, and life satisfaction (Emmons, 2016). Spiritual health is about connecting with yourself, trusting yourself, believing in yourself, and most importantly giving yourself.

Key Aspects of Spiritual Health

Mindfulness and Meditation: It is not just for monks. These practices promote self-awareness, reduce stress, and deepen one's connection to purpose (Kabat-Zinn, 2015). Things like cleaning and organizing our great ways forms of meditation.

Gratitude Practice: Reflecting on gratitude cultivates a positive mindset and emotional well-being (Emmons, 2016). Be thankful, even if it is hard.

Connection with Nature: Spending time outdoors reduces stress and promotes emotional balance (APA, 2022). Opt outside and connect with the earth.

Exercise: Cultivating Spiritual Well-Being

Daily Gratitude Practice: List three things you are grateful for each day.

Mindfulness Walk: Spend time in nature, focusing on each sensation and the calming effects of the natural world.

Breathwork Practice: Practicing deep breathing brings a sense of calm and connection, advancing mental clarity and focus. Take a breath.

Reflective Question:
How does connecting with your purpose support your journey toward a fulfilling and purposeful life?

Challenge yourself: What bold action can you take today to step beyond the ordinary?

Practical Steps: Integrating Health and Well-Being into Daily Life

Achieving well-being does not require drastic changes but rather the gradual incorporation of habits that support body, mind, and spirit. Here are some practical strategies for integrating health and well-being into daily life.

Develop a Routine: Routines create discipline and structure, supporting physical and mental health over the long term.

Set Measurable Health Goals: Small, specific health goals, like improving sleep or daily movement, will advance overall well-being.

Practice Mindfulness: Incorporating meditation, breathing exercises, or yoga promotes mental clarity and emotional balance.

Reflective Exercise: Defining Your Health Goals

Write Down One Physical, Mental, and Spiritual Health Goal: Outline simple action steps for each goal and track your weekly progress.

Reflect on Progress: Reflect weekly on how these practices enhance your life and support your journey toward fulfillment.

Kathleen Vohs' research highlights the role of self-control in perseverance. Her studies show that self-regulation can be strengthened like a muscle, enabling individuals to persist through challenges and achieve significant goals over time (Vohs et al., 2008).

Reflective Question:

Health and well-being are not luxuries but essentials on the path to fulfillment. How will you prioritize health in your journey toward your ideal self?

PILLAR THREE

Relationships

The Threads that Weave

"The quality of your life is the quality of your relationships."

— *Tony Robbins*

The Importance of Connection

Human beings are wired for connection. At our core, we have a profound need for relationships that ground us, nurture us, and give us a sense of belonging. Psychologists Roy Baumeister and Mark Leary (1995) found that this drive for connection is not merely a preference but a fundamental aspect of human nature. Our relationships shape our emotional and mental well-being, influencing not only how we perceive the world but also how we see ourselves. In many ways, relationships function as mirrors, reflecting our strengths, vulnerabilities, and areas for growth. When we prioritize and invest in meaningful connections, we create an environment that promotes our development and fulfillment, adding depth and purpose to our lives.

"For those of us who've struggled to connect, past experiences or fears create current barriers. But real connection is not about being flawless; it is about being authentic, showing up even when it feels vulnerable. I encourage you to see relationships as opportunities for growth, where each connection becomes a mirror that reflects your strengths and areas for resilience. The more you open yourself to others, the more you'll see the power in embracing yourself."

– E

Carol Dweck's expanded research into mindset demonstrates that a *growth mindset* is particularly impactful during periods of adversity. Individuals who view challenges as opportunities for growth and effort as a path to mastery are more likely to persevere and achieve extraordinary outcomes (Blackwell et al., 2007).

The Role of Relationships as Catalysts for Growth

When we nurture our relationships, we create opportunities for self-discovery. Relationships offer us a mirror in which we can see both our strengths and weaknesses, encouraging a balanced understanding of who we are. For instance, a close friend might tell you something you were not aware of, while a partner may challenge you to confront fears or insecurities you had not faced. This dynamic of growth and reflection makes relationships invaluable to our Pillars, helping us expand into more authentic versions of ourselves.

Social Support as a Buffer in Difficult Times

Having people to lean on creates a sense of security and belonging that supports our mental health. When we feel understood and supported, we are better equipped to manage life's difficulties, making us less likely to feel isolated or overwhelmed. This sense of connection is more than a luxury, it is a fundamental need. As psychologist Abraham Maslow (1943) pointed out in his hierarchy of needs, a sense of belonging is essential for our overall well-being. Without it, our mental health and happiness can suffer, underscoring the power of relationships as essential components of a fulfilled life.

The Physical and Emotional Benefits of Connection

The benefits of relationships extend beyond emotional support, they also have a measurable impact on our physical health. Research shows that people with strong social connections tend to live longer, experience fewer health problems, and recover more quickly from illnesses. This phenomenon is partly due to the stress-relieving effects of social interactions. When we spend time with loved ones, our bodies release oxytocin, a hormone that reduces stress and promotes feelings of calm and contentment. We start to relax. Studies also suggest that people with supportive relationships have lower levels of cortisol, the stress hormone, which has protective effects on heart health and immune function.

Reflective Question:
How do the relationships in your life support or challenge you on your journey to personal growth?

"Building meaningful relationships hasn't always been easy. My journey involved learning how to trust others and open up, even when vulnerability felt like a risk. I have come to realize that meaningful connections do not just happen, they are built through shared effort and a willingness to show up, even when it is uncomfortable. I have been fortunate to have lifelong friends to support me on my journey. If you have ever felt distant or

disconnected, remember that the best relationships often grow from honesty and patience. You're not alone, turns out we are all feeling the same way, you're allowed to take small steps toward connection."

– E

Building Healthy Relationships

Building strong, healthy relationships requires intentionality, patience, and consistent effort. These connections do not arise by chance but are cultivated through mutual respect, shared experiences, and a commitment to growth. Let us examine key elements that contribute to the foundation of nurturing and sustaining healthy, fulfilling relationships.

PERCEPTION OF A NEGATIVE EXPERIENCE

Building and Sustaining Meaningful Connections

Invest in Quality over Quantity

It is not the number of relationships we have but the depth of those connections that matters. A few close, supportive friends or family members can provide the stability and encouragement needed for fulfillment. By focusing on quality, we create bonds that feel secure, authentic, and fulfilling.

Practice Active Listening

Listening attentively is one of the simplest ways to strengthen relationships. By giving our full attention to others, we communicate respect and empathy, building trust and mutual understanding. Listening creates a safe space for open and honest communication, where each person feels heard and valued.

Show Appreciation Regularly

Expressing gratitude deepens connections and strengthens bonds. Taking time to appreciate the people in our lives, whether through a kind word, a small gesture, or a thoughtful note, reminds them of their importance. Acknowledging others' contributions promotes positive feelings and mutual respect, creating a more supportive relationship. Your words have power, you can use them to build people up or tear them down.

Be Vulnerable

Vulnerability is at the heart of meaningful relationships. Sharing our thoughts, fears, and dreams with trusted people opens the door to a deeper connection. Being a dreamer, when we are vulnerable, we give others permission to be open and honest as well, creating a foundation of trust and acceptance that enriches both lives.

Seek Mutual Growth

Relationships thrive when both individuals are committed to growth. Encouraging each other's aspirations, offering constructive feedback, and celebrating accomplishments together encourages a relationship that evolves and strengthens over time. By supporting each other's journeys, we create connections that are both meaningful and resilient.

The Power of Connection in Everyday Life

The positive effects of connection are not limited to close relationships; even brief, positive interactions with others can brighten our day. Simple acts like a friendly conversation with a neighbor, a smile shared with a stranger, or a chat with a colleague contribute to our sense of belonging. These small moments of connection remind us that we are part of a larger community, reinforcing our shared humanity.

In today's fast-paced, often digital world, it is easy to overlook these everyday opportunities for connection. Yet, these interactions provide an important reminder that we are never truly alone. Making a habit of kindness, eye contact, and genuine curiosity about others can create a ripple effect that enriches our lives and those around us.

The Lifelong Importance of Connection

Our relationships are integral to our lives, shaping who we are and supporting us through every phase of our journey. They act as mirrors, catalysts for growth, and sources of strength when we need them most. As research shows, connection has a profound impact on our mental and physical health, resilience, and overall happiness. By nurturing these connections, we create a life filled with meaning, love, and a sense of belonging that cannot be replaced.

Suniya Luthar's research on resilience identifies protective factors—such as social support, self-efficacy, and critical thinking skills—that buffer individuals from the negative effects of adversity. Building these factors enhances an individual's capacity to adapt and thrive (Luthar, Cicchetti, & Becker, 2000).

In nurturing our relationships, we invest in more than just companionship; we are investing in our own growth, resilience, and fulfillment. Whether it is family, friends, partners, or community, the people we connect with lift us, support us, and help us reach our fullest potential. In a world that can sometimes feel isolated, relationships remind us that we are all interconnected, with the ability to uplift one another in ways that truly matter.

Communication: The Heart of Connection

Open and honest communication is at the heart of any thriving relationship. Communication involves both sharing our thoughts and actively listening to others, creating an environment where each person feels valued and understood. Studies show that effective communication—especially empathetic listening—enhances bonds and helps resolve conflicts constructively (Gottman & Silver, 2015). Empathetic listening, which involves focusing on the speaker without judgment, helps build trust and reinforces understanding.

Case Study: Bridging Gaps Through Effective Communication

Consider Lisa and Tom, a couple frequently in conflict over financial matters. They realized that much of their discord stemmed from poor communication habits, with each partner focusing more on winning arguments than understanding the other. After a counseling session, they learned active listening techniques and practiced "I" statements to express feelings without blame. By applying these tools, they transformed their relationship, moving from a place of confrontation to mutual respect and empathy. This case highlights how communication skills can bridge gaps and encourages relational harmony.

Albert Bandura's *self-efficacy theory* demonstrates that belief in one's ability to influence outcomes is critical for perseverance and success. High self-efficacy promotes resilience by motivating individuals to persist through setbacks and achieve challenging goals (Bandura, 1977).

Reflective Exercise:
Think of a relationship where communication could be elevated. What steps could you take to enhance understanding and openness in that relationship?

Vulnerability: Promoting Depth and Trust

Vulnerability, the willingness to share our fears, insecurities, and authentic selves, serves as a gateway to deeper connection. Brené Brown's research emphasizes that vulnerability is not a weakness but a strength, creating pathways for trust and intimacy (Brown, 2012). When we allow ourselves to be vulnerable, we invite others to do the same, resulting in a mutual sense of safety and understanding.

Case Study: Strength in Vulnerability

After her divorce, Karen felt disconnected from her friends and isolated from her support network. When she finally opened up about her fears and challenges, her friends responded with understanding and support. This openness not only strengthened her existing friendships but also empowered her to rebuild her life. Karen's story illustrates how vulnerability can transform relationships, turning them into sources of strength and resilience.

Reflective Question:
Are their areas in your life where being vulnerable might deepen your relationships? What could you share to encourage trust and connection?

Challenge yourself: What bold action can you take today to step beyond the ordinary?

Support and Encouragement: Building a Cycle of Positivity

Offering support and encouragement, especially during challenging times, strengthens bonds and encourages positive reinforcement. According to Barbara Fredrickson's broaden-and-build theory, positive social interactions expand our mental and emotional resources, contributing to personal resilience and growth (Fredrickson, 2004). Supporting others in their journey not only benefits them but also builds our own sense of purpose and fulfillment.

Edward Deci and Richard Ryan's *self-determination theory* emphasizes the importance of intrinsic motivation in overcoming adversity. People who feel autonomous, competent, and connected are more likely to stay motivated and resilient when pursuing long-term goals (Deci & Ryan, 1985).

Exercise: Creating a Supportive Cycle

Identify One Person in Need: Think of someone who could benefit from encouragement or support in your life.

Offer Support: It could be a thoughtful message, listening to them without judgment, or expressing appreciation for their efforts.

Reflect on the Interaction: Consider how this act of support affects your relationship and your sense of fulfillment.

Quality Time: Building Shared Experiences

Dedicating quality time to relationships is essential yet often challenging in today's busy world. Studies indicate that time spent in meaningful interactions significantly affects relationship satisfaction and strengthens bonds (Sprecher, 2014). Quality time extends beyond simply spending hours together; it involves engaging in shared activities that promotes connection, laughter, and understanding.

Case Study: Rekindling Connection through Quality Time

James and Emily, both balancing careers and parenting, realized that their relationship was growing distant. They decided to schedule regular "date nights" to reconnect. These evenings, where they would put away their phones and focus solely on each other, allowed them to rebuild intimacy and deepen their connection. Their experience underscores that even small, intentional efforts to spend quality time together can enhance relationship health.

> **Reflective Question:**
> **What activities or rituals can you implement to ensure quality time with those who matter most?**
>
> **Challenge yourself: What bold action can you take today to step beyond the ordinary?**

Mutual Respect and Boundaries: Creating a Safe Space

Mutual respect and clear boundaries are fundamental for a healthy relationship dynamic. Boundaries empower individuals to communicate their limits and protect their well-being. Research shows that honoring boundaries within relationships reduces conflict and promotes trust (Baucom & Epstein, 2016). Setting boundaries may involve simple agreements on personal space, privacy, or topics that feel sensitive. By establishing boundaries, we create a secure foundation that promotes harmony and growth.

Exercise: Boundary Setting for Healthier Relationships

Identify Key Boundaries: Reflect on areas where your limits may feel compromised.

Communicate Your Needs: Share these boundaries clearly and respectfully with the people involved.

Respect Others' Boundaries: Practice honoring the boundaries others have set for themselves.

Expressing Gratitude: Strengthening Bonds Through Appreciation

Expressing gratitude is a simple yet profound way to strengthen relationships. Research shows that individuals who frequently express gratitude feel more satisfied and connected (Algoe et al., 2010). Simple acts of appreciation, such as acknowledging someone's kindness or thanking them for their support, reinforce positive feelings and promote an environment of trust and warmth.

Exercise: Daily Practice of Gratitude

Identify Three People: Choose three individuals in your life whom you appreciate.

Express Your Gratitude: Write a message, make a call, or have a conversation to express your appreciation.

Reflect on the Impact: Observe how this act of gratitude influences your relationship with each person.

Reflective Question:
How can you make expressing gratitude a regular part of your interactions, and how might it impact your relationships?

Challenge yourself: What bold action can you take today to step beyond the ordinary?

The Role of Relationships on Your Journey

Relationships are crucial to personal growth and development. Psychologists have found that individuals often adopt the values, attitudes, and behaviors of those they associate with, a principle known as social learning theory (Bandura, 1977). Positive relationships inspire us to work toward our goals and promote a growth-oriented mindset. Mentors, role models, and supportive friends provide guidance, accountability, and encouragement, enriching our journey toward self-fulfillment.

Case Study: Mentorship as a Catalyst for Growth

John, an aspiring entrepreneur, struggled with self-doubt and lacked direction. His mentor's influence, providing practical guidance and emotional support, helped him develop confidence and clarity. John's journey highlights the transformative impact that mentorship and role models can have on personal growth by offering wisdom, encouragement, and motivation.

Emmy Werner's longitudinal study on at-risk children found that resilience is not an inherent trait but rather the result of strong relationships and supportive environments. This research highlights the importance of promoting external resources alongside internal grit (Werner, 1989).

Reflective Question:
Who are the mentors or role models in your life, and how have they contributed to your personal development?

Relationships and Community: Expanding Connection Beyond the Individual

Engaging with our communities expands our understanding of relationships and enhances our lives on a broader scale. Community involvement provides a sense of belonging and purpose, reinforcing shared goals and values (Putnam, 2000). Community engagement, through volunteering, joining local groups, or attending shared interest events, strengthens both individual and collective growth.

Engagement and Belonging

Engaging in community activities nurtures personal and collective well-being by building purpose and a sense of responsibility. Participating in local initiatives allows us to connect with people who share similar interests, reinforcing bonds and enhancing mental health.

Reflective Question:
How does being part of a community support your personal growth and sense of purpose?

Challenge yourself: What bold action can you take today to step beyond the ordinary?

The Ripple Effect of Relationships

Investing in relationships creates a ripple effect, impacting not only our lives but also our families, communities, and organizations. In family dynamics, nurturing healthy relationships promotes empathy, resilience, and positive social skills in children, providing them with a foundation of trust and support (Bowlby, 1988). In communities, strong relationships build cohesion and collaboration, leading to enhanced social resilience and productivity (Putnam, 2000).

Relationships in the Workplace

In professional settings, encouraging positive relationships among team members encourages collaboration, creativity, and job satisfaction. Studies indicate that workplaces with supportive relationships report higher morale, reduced turnover, and increased productivity (Dutton & Heaphy, 2003). When individuals feel valued and supported, they are more likely to contribute meaningfully to the organization's success.

Reflective Exercise:
List the relationships that positively impact your life. Reflect on how each connection contributes to your growth and fulfillment.

Weaving a Fulfilled Life

Relationships are the threads that weave our lives together, providing essential support, encouragement, and inspiration. Prioritizing healthy relationships and community connections enriches our journey toward fulfillment. By consciously cultivating relationships that align with our values and growth goals, we create a support network that empowers us on our path to becoming our ideal selves.

Final Reflection

Consider the relationships that contribute to your personal growth. Are there connections that uplift, challenge, or inspire you? Are there relationships that require nurturing or reevaluation? By investing in connections that align with your values, you cultivate a cycle of growth, positivity, and mutual support that enhances your life and impacts those around you.

PILLAR FOUR

Career and Purpose

Navigating the Path

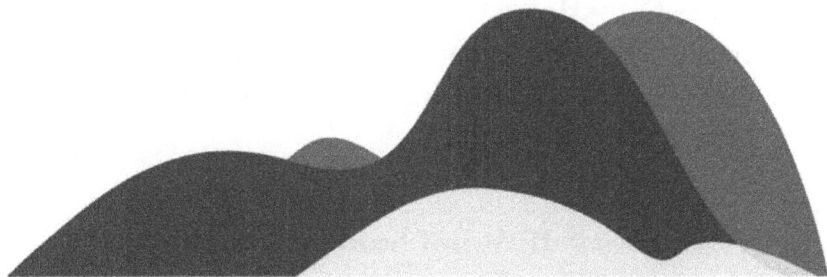

*"Your purpose in life is to find your purpose and give
your whole heart and soul to it."*

— Buddha

The pillar of career and purpose plays a vital role in shaping our sense of fulfillment and identity. Our careers are more than just a means to earn a living; they serve as powerful vehicles for personal growth, avenues to impact others, and reflections of our values and aspirations. When we align our work with our passions, we create a sense of purpose that enriches our lives and empowers us on our journey toward fulfillment (Steger et al., 2012). A purpose-driven career builds resilience, promotes motivation, and enhances life satisfaction, illustrating how meaningful work is fundamental to a well-rounded, fulfilling life (Wrzesniewski et al., 1997).

Behavioral economist Dan Ariely's experiments on intrinsic motivation showed that people are more likely to succeed when their goals align with personal meaning and purpose (Ariely, 2010).

Reflective Question:
How does your career align with your passions and values, and what steps can you take to increase that alignment?

Challenge yourself: What bold action can you take today to step beyond the ordinary?

"For years, I felt lost to the roles I was expected to play, the role I put on myself. But over time, purpose comes when you let go of what you 'should' do and start exploring what genuinely drives you. I had to confront

my doubts and allow myself to pivot—choosing to embrace uncertainty rather than avoid it. Remember, a fulfilling career is not about fitting into a mold. It's about breaking free from expectations and creating something that aligns with who you are becoming."

– E

Discovering Your Purpose

Purpose is deeply personal and unique to each of us, and discovering it often requires us to turn inward. This process is not about finding a single "correct" answer; instead, it is a journey of self-exploration and growth. It calls for introspection, reflection, and a willingness to understand what truly brings us joy and fulfillment. Here are some ways to deepen this journey of discovering your purpose.

"Our careers and sense of purpose are often shaped by both our strengths and our struggles. I used to believe that a 'perfect' career path is reserved for those without setbacks, but the reality is that purpose often emerges from obstacles. Let us explore how challenges can be your greatest teachers, leading you to a path that aligns with your true self. Let your setbacks guide you, showing you what matters and shaping a career that feels deeply personal."

-E

RESISTANCE   ACCEPTANCE

The Power of Self-Reflection in Purpose Discovery

Self-reflection is at the core of understanding your purpose. When we take the time to consider what drives us, we gain a clearer view of our values, strengths, and interests. Purpose is often tied to our core values—those principles and beliefs that matter most to us. Identifying these values can provide clarity about what truly brings meaning and satisfaction into our lives.

Consider reflecting on questions like:

- What activities make me lose track of time? Activities that engross you and make hours feel like minutes often reveal a natural passion or interest.

- What causes or issues am I deeply enthusiastic about? Causes that spark a strong emotional response can signal purpose, as these are often areas where we feel compelled to make a difference.

- How can my skills make a difference? Aligning your skills with causes that matter to you allows you to contribute uniquely and meaningfully.

Exploring Your Values, Passions, and Strengths

<u>Values:</u> Our values reflect what we hold dear in life, and they shape our decisions, behavior, and interactions. Reflect on moments in your life where you felt deeply fulfilled or particularly proud. What values were you honoring in those moments? These could be values like integrity, compassion, creativity, or growth. Defining these values can guide you in choosing a career path or projects that align with your purpose.

<u>Passions:</u> Passion often points toward purpose. Think about topics, hobbies, or issues that you feel strongly about or that evoke a deep sense of excitement or curiosity. For example, if you feel enthusiastic about environmental conservation, your purpose might involve a career in sustainability, environmental advocacy, or eco-friendly product development. Passion fuels motivation, making even the most challenging tasks more enjoyable.

<u>Strengths:</u> Purpose is not just about doing what we love—it is about contributing in ways that come naturally to us. Reflect on your strengths and unique talents. What are you naturally good at, and how do these strengths add value to others? Your purpose often lies at the intersection of what you love and at what you are skilled. For instance, a natural communicator who loves health advocacy might find

purpose in health coaching or public speaking on wellness topics.

Finding Patterns Through Reflection

Once you have explored your values, passions, and strengths, take some time to look for patterns. Purpose often reveals itself through recurring themes and common threads in our lives. Reflect on past experiences, roles, and projects that brought you fulfillment, and consider how these elements might connect. Did you feel purposeful when you were mentoring others? Or perhaps you felt a deep sense of purpose when working on creative projects or helping others in crisis. Recognizing these patterns can offer valuable clues to the work that will feel meaningful to you in the long run.

Questions to Help Identify Purpose

- What brings me joy and fulfillment? Consider both work and personal activities that leave you feeling accomplished and happy.

- What have I overcome, and how can I help others through similar challenges? Many find purpose in helping others with struggles they have faced and conquered.

- How would I spend my time if money were not a concern? When we remove financial limitations from the equation, we often discover our truest interests.

- What legacy do I want to leave? Thinking about the impact you want to make can clarify what matters most to you.

Each of these questions helps you move closer to uncovering a purpose that is authentic and enduring. Purpose evolves as we do, so re-visiting these questions periodically ensures your career stays aligned with who you are becoming.

Taking Action to Discover Purpose

Discovering purpose is not solely an internal journey, it is also about acting. Experiment with activities, projects, or even volunteer work that aligns with your values and passions. Sometimes, it is only through action that we utterly understand what resonates with us. Evaluate different paths and reflect on how each experience feels. Did it bring fulfillment, challenge you, or reveal a new interest? Treat this exploration as a journey rather than a destination.

Volunteer or Mentor: Offering your time to causes you care about can help you connect to what feels meaningful. Giving yourself to something other than yourself. Whether it is mentoring young people, supporting community events, or working with non-profits, these experiences can be invaluable.

Pursue Passion Projects: Sometimes our purpose is not tied to our career directly. If you have a passion or hobby, dedicate time to it, and notice how it impacts your life. For example, if you love writing, start a blog, or if you enjoy helping others, consider part-time coaching or consulting.

Seek New Experiences: Step outside your comfort zone to experience new environments, perspectives, or roles. Exposure to the latest ideas and people can reveal unexpected interests and potential career paths that align with your purpose.

Embracing the Evolution of Purpose

Purpose is not static. As we grow and change, our purpose often evolves with us. It is common for people to have multiple purposes throughout separate phases of their lives. For instance, you might start with a purpose focused on personal success or mastery, and later find fulfillment in mentoring others or contributing to social causes. Embracing this evolution allows us to stay open to new opportunities that align with our personal and professional growth.

Case Study: Finding Purpose Through Personal Interests

Alex, a graphic designer, initially took on projects only for financial stability. However, he found himself drawn to projects related to environmental sustainability. This realization led him to shift his focus toward eco-friendly organizations, aligning his work with his values. His new focus not only increased his job satisfaction but also gave him a sense of contributing to a cause he cared about. Alex's journey shows how discovering purpose through self-reflection can transform a career from routine to fulfilling.

Reflective Exercise:
Take 10 minutes to list activities, causes, and issues that make you feel energized and fulfilled. Reflect on how these can be integrated into your career.

Aligning Career with Purpose

Once you understand your purpose, the next step is aligning your career with it. This alignment makes work more than a paycheck; it turns it into a source of inspiration. As poet Rumi said, "Let yourself be silently drawn by the strange pull of what you really love. It will not lead you astray." Research supports this idea, showing that alignment between career and values leads to higher job satisfaction, engagement, and productivity (May et al., 2004).

Steps to Align Your Career with Purpose

Define Your Core Values: Identify the principles that guide your life. Whether it is creativity, empathy, or innovation, knowing your core values will help you seek roles and companies that reflect those ideals.

Research Purpose-Driven Companies: Look for organizations that prioritize social responsibility, sustainability, or employee well-being. Working for a company with a clear mission that resonates with your values enhances career satisfaction.

<u>Seek Roles that Encourage Growth</u>: Pursue opportunities that challenge you and offer avenues for developing new skills. Continuous learning promotes a sense of purpose and self-determination, which are key to job satisfaction (Deci & Ryan, 2000).

Case Study: Aligning Work with Personal Values

Leah, a marketing manager, felt a disconnect between her role and her values. By actively seeking a position in a nonprofit that focused on educational access, she found a role that allowed her to use her skills to promote equity. This shift elevated her job satisfaction and gave her a renewed sense of purpose. Leah's story illustrates how aligning a career with one's values can lead to meaningful and fulfilling work.

Reflective Question:
How do your current career goals align with your personal values, and what changes might strengthen that alignment?

Challenge yourself: What bold action can you take today to step beyond the ordinary?

Seeking Opportunities for Growth

Pursuing growth opportunities is crucial for creating a fulfilling career aligned with your purpose. Taking on roles and projects that challenge you promotes resilience, deepens knowledge, and adds meaning to your work. According to Deci and Ryan's self-determination theory, learning and mastering new skills promote self-determination and purpose, enhancing both personal and professional satisfaction (Deci & Ryan, 2000).

CHASING
OPPORTUNITY

ATTRACTING
OPPORTUNITIES

Stevan Hobfoll's conservation of resources theory shows that resilience is enhanced by accumulating and protecting resources—whether emotional, social, or material. People with access to multiple resources are better equipped to recover and thrive after setbacks (Hobfoll, 1989).

Case Study: Growth Through Professional Challenges

After working as a software developer for five years, Aaron felt stagnant. He started volunteering for cross-functional projects within his company, which allowed him to develop leadership skills. This experience not only revitalized his career but also aligned it with his values of learning and community engagement. Aaron's journey highlights how pursuing growth within your role can lead to greater fulfillment.

Exercise: Identifying Growth Opportunities

List Three Skills: Identify three skills you would like to develop.

Research Growth Opportunities: Look for projects, workshops, or certifications that can enhance these skills.

Commit to One Action: Set a timeline for acquiring these skills or completing these experiences and track your progress.

Reflective Question:
What steps can you take to ensure continuous growth in your current career?

Embracing Change

Embracing change in your career can open doors to new growth and align your work with your evolving purpose. Research shows that individuals who make bold career changes in pursuit of their passions report higher satisfaction, even if the path is unconventional (Hall & Chandler, 2005). Although change can be intimidating, it often leads to greater opportunities when aligned with core values.

Case Study: A Career Pivot Inspired by Purpose

Mark had a stable career in finance but felt unfulfilled. Drawn to education, he decided to transition into teaching. Despite the challenges, he found the work more rewarding and purposeful. His shift demonstrates how bold career moves, when driven by purpose, can lead to a more satisfying and impactful career.

Reflective Exercise:
Reflect on areas in your career where change might benefit you. What adjustments could bring you closer to work that aligns with your values?

Network and Collaborate

Surrounding yourself with like-minded professionals provides support, inspiration, and opportunities for growth. Building a network with people who share similar values creates a sense of community, belonging, and motivation (Putnam, 2000). Collaborating with others who share your passions reinforces your purpose and provides fresh perspectives.

Daniel Pink, in *Drive: The Surprising Truth About What Motivates Us*, argues that intrinsic motivation thrives when individuals have autonomy over their tasks, opportunities for mastery, and a sense of purpose in their work. These factors drive sustained success and satisfaction (Pink, 2009)

Tips for Building a Purpose-Driven Network

<u>Attend Industry Events</u>: Participating in events related to your field connects you with people who share your interests. Strike up a conversation at the gym or at the local coffee shop.

<u>Join Purpose-Aligned Groups</u>: Networking within organizations that focus on issues you are passionate about can deepen your sense of purpose. There are countless groups to choose from, groups like this can bring pride and purpose.

<u>Seek Out Mentors</u>: Mentors who share your values provide guidance and inspiration, helping you navigate your career path. The local college or successful business, strike up a conversation. Who knows where that might lead?

Case Study: Building a Supportive Professional Network

Sarah, a social worker passionate about mental health, joined a local group for mental health advocates. This network offered her resources, collaboration opportunities, and new friendships that reinforced her commitment to her field. Sarah's experience shows how building a professional network can sustain motivation and support a purpose-driven career.

Reflective Question:
How can you expand your network to include
more individuals who align with your career goals
and values?

Challenge yourself: What bold action can you take
today to step beyond the ordinary?

Make Purpose a Daily Practice

Aligning your career with purpose is an ongoing process, not a one-time decision. Integrating purpose into daily practices—by setting intentions, reflecting on tasks, and appreciating small achievements—keeps you connected to your larger goals. Research indicates that individuals who find purpose in their daily work report higher resilience and job satisfaction (Wrzesniewski et al., 1997)

PURPOSE

WITH

WITHOUT

Daily Practice Suggestions:

Set Morning Intentions: Each day, reflect on how your work can contribute to your purpose. If it is not, you must find time to work towards your own goals.

Celebrate Small Wins: Acknowledge the daily efforts that align with your purpose. Life is about the journey, celebrating the trip, not the destination.

Practice Gratitude: Regularly remind yourself of the positive impact your work has on others. Some people love and support you. Let them know you care.

Reflective Question:
How can you incorporate purpose-driven practices into your daily routine to enhance your sense of fulfillment?

Giving Back and Creating Impact

Making a difference in others' lives transforms a career from self-centered to purpose centered. When we focus on impact, we work with a sense of significance and contribution. Studies show that those who help others through their work report higher job satisfaction and motivation (Grant, 2007).

Behavioral economist Dan Ariely's experiments on intrinsic motivation showed that people are more likely to succeed when their goals align with personal meaning and purpose (Ariely, 2010).

Case Study: Promoting Fulfillment Through Giving Back

John, a corporate lawyer, began volunteering his legal expertise to support nonprofits. This experience enriched his sense of purpose, giving his career renewed meaning. John's story demonstrates how giving back through your career can deepen fulfillment.

Exercise: Identifying Ways to Give Back

Consider Your Skills: Reflect on how your unique skills can serve others.

Identify Opportunities: Look for volunteer roles, mentorship possibilities, or community involvement that aligns with your values.

Commit to Impact: Start with one small act that allows you to contribute positively.

Reflective Question:
What small steps can you take to incorporate giving back into your career?

Challenge yourself: What bold action can you take today to step beyond the ordinary?

Overcoming Common Career Challenges

<u>Handling Setbacks</u>: Setbacks can be discouraging, but they are also opportunities to gain experience and grow. Reflect on what these moments teach you and how they align with your purpose. Be resilient.

<u>Maintaining Work-Life Balance</u>: Work-life balance is key to long-term fulfillment. Boundaries, self-care, and intentional scheduling help maintain well-being while pursuing meaningful work (Greenhaus & Powell, 2006). It is your responsibility to protect your work-life balance. We have all seen work take over someone's life.

<u>Dealing with Uncertainty</u>: Careers are rarely linear. Embracing uncertainty builds resilience, adaptability, and openness to new opportunities (Baumeister, 2005). Be bold, you can fail if you do not quit.

Edwin Locke and Gary Latham's *goal-setting theory* demonstrates that specific, challenging goals tied to personal values are more effective in sustaining motivation than vague or extrinsic objectives. Clear goals promote focus, effort, and persistence (Locke & Latham, 1990).

Reflective Exercise:
List a recent career challenge and consider the growth lessons it provided. How did it align or misalign with your purpose, and what adjustments can you make for the future?

Achieving Work-Life Balance

Work-life balance supports sustainable well-being, allowing us to engage fully in our careers while preserving time for personal life, relationships, and self-care. Studies indicate that those who prioritize balance experience lower stress, better mental health, and greater life satisfaction (Maslach & Leiter, 2016).

Strategies for Maintaining Balance

Set Clear Boundaries: Define work hours and commit to "clocking out" mentally and physically.

Practice Time Management: Effective time management reduces work encroachment on personal time, increasing satisfaction.

Negotiate Flexibility: Advocate for flexible arrangements that support both work and personal goals.

Pursue Joy Outside of Work: Engaging in non-work activities enhances happiness, refreshes the mind, and strengthens work motivation.

Deci and Richard Ryan's research on self-determination theory emphasizes that intrinsic motivation stemming from personal interest or enjoyment leads to higher engagement and success compared to extrinsic motivators like rewards or punishments (Deci & Ryan, 1985).

Case Study: Finding Balance as a Key to Fulfillment

Rachel, a physician, found herself nearing burnout. By setting clear boundaries and scheduling self-care, she restored her work-life balance, which elevated her job satisfaction and overall well-being. Her experience shows that balance is essential for long-term fulfillment.

Reflective Question:
What strategies can you implement to create a sustainable work-life balance that aligns with your values?

Challenge yourself: What bold action can you take today to step beyond the ordinary?

Personal Development Practices for Career Growth:

Embrace Continuous Learning: Seek education and skill-building to stay adaptable and innovative.

Set Goals: Clear, achievable goals provide motivation and encourage a sense of accomplishment.

Reflect Regularly: Regular reflection encourages self-awareness and personal growth, enhancing professional performance.

Navigating Your Path to Fulfillment

In the journey toward a meaningful life, career, and purpose act as essential guides, helping us realize our potential. By discovering our purpose, aligning our work with our passions, and committing to positive impact, we create a career that fuels fulfillment. Career satisfaction enhances life satisfaction, underscoring its importance in personal fulfillment (Judge et al., 1998). Consider how your career aligns with your values and passions. Are you taking intentional steps toward fulfilling work? Reflect on how you can further align your career with your purpose and create a life filled with meaning and impact.

PILLAR FIVE

Financial Stability

Building a Financial Foundation

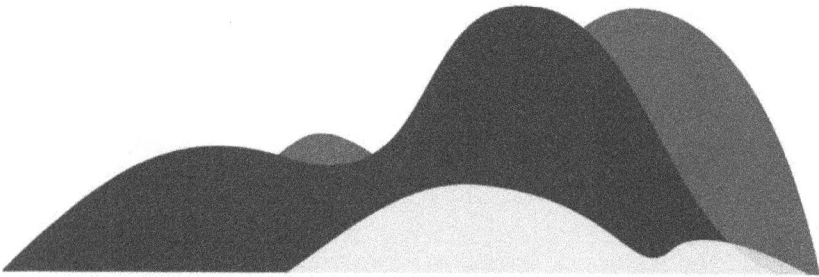

"Financial freedom is available to those who learn about it and work for it."

— Robert Kiyosaki

Disclaimer

While financial stability is an essential pillar for building a balanced and fulfilling life, the information in this chapter is intended as general advice for educational purposes. Monetary management is highly personal and involves complex factors unique to everyone's circumstances, goals, and lifestyle. This chapter provides strategies, examples, and insights to encourage readers to think deeply about their finances, set personal goals, and adopt healthy financial habits. However, it does not replace professional financial advice tailored to individual needs.

For personalized guidance, it is always wise to consult a certified financial advisor or other qualified financial professional. Financial experts can offer specific recommendations on budgeting, investments, retirement planning, debt management, and other financial considerations that may not be covered fully here. Collaborating directly with a financial advisor can help ensure that your approach aligns with your risk tolerance, long-term goals, and any specific challenges you may face.

The Value of Financial Stability in a Fulfilling Life

Financial stability is foundational to a balanced, fulfilling life. It supports other pillars of well-being by reducing stress, providing freedom, and empowering individuals to pursue goals and dreams without constant financial worry. Financial wellness is not about accumulating wealth for wealth's sake—it is about cultivating a secure foundation that enables us to live with purpose, contribute to our communities, and feel prepared for the future. Studies consistently show that financial security is closely tied to life satisfaction and mental health, underscoring its importance as a fundamental pillar of overall fulfillment (Dolan, Peasgood, & White, 2008).

Financial stability allows us to make decisions from a place of strength rather than scarcity. When we can approach life confidently, knowing we have a secure financial foundation, it impacts every other area—from career choices to personal growth and from relationships to community involvement.

Reflective Question:
What does financial stability mean to you personally, and how does it align with your overall life goals?

Challenge yourself: What bold action can you take today to step beyond the ordinary?

"My relationship with money hasn't always been secure. There were times when financial stress seemed insurmountable, but it was in these moments that I remembered my parents' teachings and realized the importance of building stability not just for comfort, but for peace of mind. Financial stability is not about wealth; it is about empowering yourself to live without the constant weight of worry. If you've ever felt limited by financial constraints, know that small, consistent actions can create a foundation that sustains you, giving you the freedom to focus on what truly matters."

– E

Understanding Financial Stability

Achieving financial stability involves building a secure financial base that allows for effective management of daily expenses, planning for future needs, and investing in personal and professional growth. Financial stability is not about achieving a fixed financial milestone; it is about developing habits and practices that create long-term security and peace of mind. Here are several key components:

Creating and Sticking to a Budget

A well-structured budget is the backbone of financial stability. Budgeting offers clarity on income, expenses, and priorities, empowering individuals to make informed choices that align with their values and goals. Research links financial planning, including budgeting, to higher financial well-being and reduced stress, as it helps individuals live within their means and allocate resources effectively (Lusardi & Mitchell, 2014).

A monthly budget allows us to:

Prioritize essential spending: Ensuring that basic needs are met before luxury expenses.

Allocate savings and debt repayment: Setting aside funds for an emergency fund, retirement, and investments.

Track progress toward financial goals: Monitoring spending and adjusting as needed.

Case Study: Reclaiming Financial Control through Budgeting

Maria, a young professional, struggled with managing her finances and ended up accumulating credit card debt due to impulsive spending. She decided to create a monthly budget, breaking down her expenses into needs, wants, and savings. By tracking her spending, she could prioritize paying off debt, and within a year, she had built a modest emergency fund. Maria's experience shows that budgeting can be transformative, encouraging discipline and financial freedom.

Exercise: Building Your First Budget

Step 1: List all sources of income.

Step 2: Break down monthly expenses into essential (housing, food) and discretionary (dining, entertainment).

Step 3: Set aside a percentage for debt repayment and savings.

Step 4: Track and adjust each month to ensure goals are met.

Reflective Question:
How can budgeting help you better align your financial decisions with your personal values?

Building and Maintaining an Emergency Fund

Research shows that households with emergency savings report greater life satisfaction and reduced stress, as financial security helps individuals manage life's uncertainties (Garman & Forgue, 2011).

Case Study: Building Peace of Mind with an Emergency Fund

James, a freelancer, struggled with the unpredictability of his income. He decided to save three months of living expenses to create stability. When a client delayed payment for two months, his emergency fund enabled him to cover his bills without borrowing. James's experience illustrates how an emergency fund can reduce anxiety and promote stability.

Exercise: Starting an Emergency Fund

Set a Goal: Start small by aiming to save one month's worth of essential expenses.

Automate Contributions: Set up an automatic transfer to a dedicated savings account each month.

Evaluate Monthly: Track your progress and celebrate each milestone to keep motivated.

Reflective Question:
How would having an emergency fund impact your sense of security and peace of mind?

Challenge yourself: What bold action can you take today to step beyond the ordinary?

Strategic Debt Management

Effectively managing debt is essential to financial well-being. Excessive debt, especially high-interest debt, is intricately linked to stress and can affect mental health (Sweet et al., 2013). Financial experts distinguish between "good" debt (mortgages, student loans) that can serve as investments in future growth and "bad" debt (high-interest credit cards), which can hinder financial progress.

Managing debt involves creating a structured repayment plan:

- Focus on high-interest debts first to reduce financial strain.

- Consider debt consolidation to lower interest rates and simplify payments.

- Maintain regular payments to elevate credit scores and reduce financial pressure.

Case Study: Breaking Free from Debt

Lisa, who had accumulated credit card debt from unexpected medical expenses, felt overwhelmed by her financial obligations. She implemented a debt snowball strategy, focusing on her smallest debt first and working her way up. As her debts reduced, she felt a sense of accomplishment and control over her finances. Lisa's journey highlights the value of strategic debt repayment.

Reflective Question:
What impact does manage or reducing debt have on your stress levels and financial well-being?

"Financial stability may feel out of reach for those of us who have faced financial hardships or setbacks. But this chapter is about creating stability and empowerment in

a way that does not ignore past challenges, it builds on them. Your journey toward financial well-being is uniquely yours, and the steps you take are valid, no matter how small. Each positive choice contributes to a foundation of freedom, security, and empowerment."

– E

The Role of Financial Education

Financial literacy is essential for achieving and maintaining stability. Studies show that individuals with a solid understanding of financial basics—like budgeting, saving, investing, and debt management—make better-informed choices and experience greater well-being (Lusardi & Tufano, 2009). Financial literacy is a lifelong skill that helps individuals make informed decisions, manage resources effectively, and avoid common financial pitfalls.

Enhancing Financial Literacy

Learning Financial Fundamentals

Financial education begins with mastering key concepts, such as budgeting, saving, and investing. Numerous resources, such as books, online courses, and podcasts, offer foundational knowledge.

Staying Financially Informed

The financial landscape constantly changes, influenced by new regulations, economic shifts, and market trends. Staying informed through reliable financial news sources, seminars, or workshops helps individuals adapt their strategies to current conditions.

Case Study: Empowering Through Education

Mark and Ellie, a young couple, struggled to manage their finances and felt unprepared for the future. After attending financial literacy workshops, they gained the confidence to budget effectively and plan for retirement. This educational journey transformed their financial outlook and empowered them to make informed decisions for their future.

Exercise: Boosting Financial Knowledge

Choose Two Topics: Identify two financial areas (e.g., investing, debt reduction) where you want to elevate.

Learn and Apply: Read a book, take a course, or consult an expert, then apply what you learn.

Reflect: Evaluate how these changes elevate your financial habits and reduce stress.

Reflective Question:
How can increasing your financial knowledge empower you to make choices aligned with your goals?

Freedom to Invest in Personal Growth and Well-being

Financial stability provides the freedom to invest in personal development without the constraint of financial worry. With a strong financial foundation, individuals can pursue educational opportunities, hobbies, travel, or self-care activities that enrich life. Research suggests that financial security enables continuous growth, allowing people to reach their potential without financial constraints.

Case Study: Investing in Growth through Financial Freedom

Alex, a nurse, saved over time to travel and attend medical workshops. This investment enriched her professional skills and deepened her personal sense of purpose, showcasing how financial security supports meaningful growth.

Reflective Question:
What personal growth activities would you pursue if financial constraints were minimized?

Financial Stability as a Tool for Contribution

Achieving financial security allows people to contribute to causes they care about, enhancing both personal and communal well-being. Studies show that acts of generosity, whether financial or through volunteer work, are linked to increased life satisfaction and mental health (Dunn et al., 2008).

Case Study: Giving Back with Financial Stability

Jake, a software developer, used his resources to support educational initiatives, which brought him a sense of purpose. His journey shows how financial security enables giving, enriching both personal and communal lives.

Reflective Question:
How would you like to give back, and how can financial stability support this goal?

Challenge yourself: What bold action can you take today to step beyond the ordinary?

Actionable Steps for Financial Freedom

Set Clear Financial Goals:

Define both short- and long-term objectives to create focus and motivation.

Create and Adjust a Budget:

A realistic budget that aligns with personal values is crucial for tracking and achieving financial goals.

Prioritize Saving and Investing:

Establish a habit of saving a portion of your income, aiming for at least 20% to build a secure future.

Review and Reflect Regularly:

Life circumstances change; reassess your financial goals periodically to stay aligned with evolving priorities. Stay flexible.

Reflective Exercise:
Write down a financial goal and outline steps to achieve it. Reflect monthly on your progress and any adjustments needed.

Financial Stability and the Pursuit of Fulfillment

Financial stability is a cornerstone of a fulfilling life. With a secure foundation, we are empowered to focus on other areas that bring joy, meaning, and purpose. Each step toward financial well-being moves us closer to a balanced, fulfilling life that aligns with our highest aspirations.

Consider how achieving financial stability can enhance your overall sense of well-being. What steps will you take to move closer to this goal?

PILLAR SIX

Contribution and Impact

Creating a Legacy Beyond Ourselves

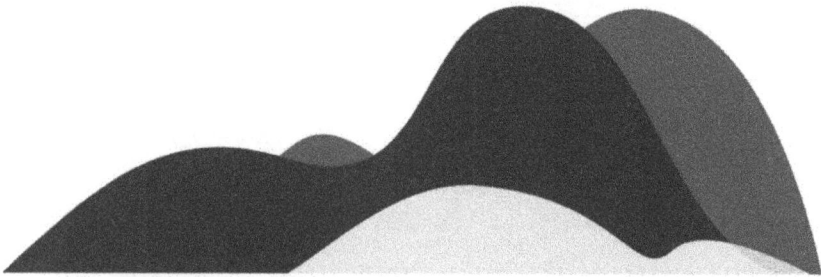

"The legacy you leave is the life you lead."

— Stephen Covey

As we strive to become our ideal selves, the journey inevitably leads us to consider our role in the larger fabric of society. Contribution and impact are essential aspects of a meaningful life; they allow us to reach beyond our aspirations and leave a positive mark on the world. Martin Seligman, a pioneer in positive psychology, captured this sentiment: "Authentic happiness comes from creating meaning and purpose." By focusing on giving back and positively impacting others, we elevate ourselves and those around us, creating a ripple effect that can transform families, communities, and even societies.

"The idea of 'making an impact' used to feel intimidating to me. I questioned how much I could really do, or if my efforts would even matter. But over time, I learned that impact does not require grandeur, it is about consistent, small acts that accumulate over time. Contribution is within your reach, no matter your circumstances. Whether you are helping one person or many, remember that each step you take creates a ripple effect. Don't underestimate the power of your actions, however small they may seem."

– E

Why Contribution and Impact Matter

The desire to be effective is deeply embedded in human nature. Our need to contribute to something greater than ourselves has been studied and reflected upon by psychologists, philosophers, and influential figures throughout history. Research in psychology shows that contributing to the welfare of others enhances life satisfaction, encourages a sense of purpose, and strengthens our connection to society (Baumeister & Leary, 1995). When we channel our skills, talents, and time in ways that benefit others, we not only create a positive impact on those around us but also experience a profound sense of fulfillment.

Contribution is about more than grand gestures or formal volunteering; it is about the small, intentional choices we make each day. These moments of generosity, kindness, and service weave into the fabric of our lives, enriching both ourselves and those we help. By cultivating a mindset focused on giving, we make meaningful contributions that align with our values and strengths, building a life of purpose and impact.

The Psychological Drive to Contribute

Psychologists Roy Baumeister and Mark Leary famously theorized that human beings have a "need to belong" as a fundamental component of our psychological makeup. They argued that the drive for social connection and the desire to feel valued in a group are key factors in human happiness and well-being. In their 1995 study, they emphasized that "people have a basic psychological need to feel closely connected to others, and that caring for others plays a significant role in satisfying this need." This intrinsic desire to connect with others through contribution is what drives many of us to seek ways to positively impact our families, communities, and society.

Contributing to others brings a sense of significance to our lives, helping us feel that we are a part of something larger than ourselves. Mahatma Gandhi captured this sentiment when he said, "The best way to find yourself is to lose yourself in the service of others." This idea reflects a universal truth: when we serve, we transcend our own limitations and tap into a source of profound fulfillment and meaning. As we shift focus from "What can I gain?" to "How can I serve?" We open ourselves up to a greater sense of purpose.

"Impact isn't only for those with resources or perfect lives; it's something we can all create, starting exactly where we are. Let us explore how giving back can be an act of resilience, where we turn our challenges into a source of strength and empathy for others. Contribution is about finding meaning in every experience, good or bad, and choosing to leave a positive mark. Your impact, no matter how small, has the power to create lasting change."

- E

Gretchen Spreitzer and Jane Dutton's *thriving at work framework* reveals that individuals are most motivated when they experience vitality and learning at work. Meaningful goals and a sense of progress are critical components for encouraging intrinsic motivation (Spreitzer & Dutton, 2005).

How Contribution Enhances Life Satisfaction and Purpose

Making a positive impact on others enriches our lives in ways that go beyond material success. Research has consistently shown that individuals who give back experience heightened life satisfaction and elevated mental health. Psychologist Martin Seligman, known as the father of positive psychology, emphasized the importance of living a life of purpose through "meaningful engagement" with others. In his book Authentic Happiness, Seligman explained, "When we take active steps to enhance the well-being of others, we enhance our well-being as well."

The Many Faces of Contribution and Impact

Contribution and impact are not limited to formal volunteer work or monetary donations. They are woven into our everyday actions, choices, and interactions. Here are several dimensions through which contribution can take place:

Time and Presence: Giving our time is one of the most valuable contributions we can make. Whether it is working the 9-5, actively listening to someone who needs support, volunteering in a local community, or spending quality time with loved ones, our presence can have a profound impact. As Mother Teresa famously said, "Not all of us can do great things. But we can do small things with great love."

Skills and Talents: Sharing our unique skills and talents allows us to contribute in ways that feel authentic and meaningful. A teacher who offers extra tutoring to struggling students, a chef who cooks for a community event, or a musician who performs at a charity benefit are all examples of using one's skills to make a difference. By aligning our contributions with our strengths, we can offer something valuable that benefits others.

Resources and Financial Support: Donations, whether large or small, play an essential role in creating positive change. Philanthropy allows us to support causes we care about, from local charities to global initiatives. Andrew Carnegie, one of the most influential philanthropists of the 19th century, advocated for the importance of wealth distribution, saying, "The man who dies thus rich dies disgraced." Carnegie believed that those with the means to give had a responsibility to invest in the welfare of society.

Acts of Kindness and Compassion: Small, everyday acts of kindness can be among the most impactful forms of contribution. Holding the door open for someone, offering a smile, or expressing gratitude to those around us may seem simple, but these actions contribute to a culture of positivity and connection. As the Dalai Lama often teaches, "Be kind whenever possible. It is always possible." These small gestures collectively create a ripple effect that promotes a sense of community and belonging.

Cultivating a Mindset Focused on Contribution

Adopting a mindset centered on giving requires intentional practice. To truly embody the spirit of contribution, we must shift our focus from self-centered goals to value-driven actions that prioritize the welfare of others. This mindset shift not only helps us create a positive impact on others but also transforms how we view ourselves and our lives.

1. Reflect on Your Values

Contribution is most fulfilling when it aligns with our core values. Take time to reflect on what matters most to you and what causes resonate deeply. When you contribute to causes that align with your values, the experience feels more authentic and sustainable. As Oprah Winfrey once said, "The biggest adventure you can take is to live the life of your dreams," and when our dreams include making a positive difference, the adventure becomes even richer.

2. Seek Opportunities for Everyday Giving

Contribution does not have to be elaborate. Look for small ways to help in your daily life. For example, you might offer to help a neighbor with errands, support a friend's project, or spend a few hours each month at a local organization. These small acts are the building blocks of a life dedicated to impact.

3. Connect with Like-Minded People

Surrounding yourself with people who share a commitment to making a difference can amplify your efforts and inspire you to continue giving. Community and shared purpose create a supportive environment that sustains us, even when challenges arise. As the philosopher Albert Schweitzer noted, "One thing I know: the only ones among you who will be really happy are those who will have sought and found how to serve."

The Ripple Effect of Contribution and Legacy

Contribution has a profound ripple effect, influencing not only the recipients but also inspiring others to contribute. When we give, we set an example that encourages others to do the same, creating a cycle of kindness and service that strengthens our communities and builds a legacy of compassion. Our acts of contribution, however small, plant seeds that grow into a collective impact that transcends individual efforts.

As we move through life, the legacy we leave behind reflects the contributions we have made. Stephen Covey, author of the 7 Habits of Highly Effective People, spoke to this when he said, "What you leave behind is not what is engraved in stone monuments, but what is woven into the lives of others." Our impact is not measured by accolades or wealth, but by the positive change we inspire in those we touch.

Reflective Question:
What does the idea of contribution mean to you personally, and how do you envision creating an impact in your community or beyond?

Challenge yourself: What bold action can you take today to step beyond the ordinary?

Case Study: The Power of Small Acts

Emily, a nurse, spent years giving back by offering health advice to families in her neighborhood. Although her contributions were small—simple tips on diet, exercise, and mental wellness—she noticed that her community started living healthier lives over time. Emily's story illustrates how even small acts of kindness can create a cumulative impact that benefits everyone involved.

Reflective Question:
How do you currently give back to others, and what areas of contribution resonate most with you?

Leading with Purpose: Inspiring Positive Change

Taking initiative in projects or causes that align with our values is one of the most powerful ways to make an impact. Leadership in contribution is not necessarily about formal authority but about inspiring and guiding others toward positive change. Studies show that people who actively engage in prosocial behaviors, such as volunteering or community involvement, report higher levels of well-being and fulfillment (Aknin, Dunn, & Norton, 2012).

The Role of Purpose in Leadership

Purpose-driven leadership is about making a difference that aligns with our values and personal mission. This type of leadership can manifest in many ways:

Starting a Community Initiative: Launching or organizing local projects that address community needs, like a clean-up drive or a literacy program, can have a significant impact.

Mentorship: Sharing life lessons with younger individuals or those at earlier stages in their careers provides guidance and support that can shape futures.

Advocacy for Change: Advocacy, whether for sustainability, education reform, or protection, drives societal innovation and brings communities together around shared goals.

Case Study: A Legacy of Leadership

James, a retired schoolteacher, used his free time to mentor students from the local schools. Through weekly meetings, he shared his knowledge, helped them set goals, and even arranged college tours. Over the years, several of his mentees went on to attend university and attributed much of their success to James's support. His leadership shows how mentoring can leave a legacy, changing lives one individual at a time.

Exercise: Identify a Cause to Lead

List Personal Values: Write down the values that mean the most to you.

Research Community Needs: Look for local organizations, causes, or groups that align with these values.

Plan an Initiative: Consider how you can lead, even if it is a small effort, to create positive change.

Sharing Skills to Empower Others

Each of us has unique skills that, when shared, can create significant positive outcomes for others. When we use our skills to empower those around us, we help build their capacity and create a multiplier effect of impact. Research shows that sharing knowledge and expertise, whether through teaching, mentoring, or coaching, benefits others while promoting a sense of fulfillment and belonging in ourselves (Baumeister & Leary, 1995).

Why Sharing Skills Is So Powerful

Skill-sharing is one of the most impactful ways to contribute because it creates a foundation for sustainable change. Unlike financial resources, skills enable people to help themselves and their communities, creating long-term benefits.

Enhanced Self-Efficacy: Skill-sharing boosts individuals' confidence in their abilities, empowering them to pursue goals.

Knowledge Transfer: Knowledge-sharing builds a more informed and capable community, breaking cycles of dependency.

Case Study: Empowering Through Skill-Sharing

Sarah, an architect, saw that local schools in her city had limited exposure to art and design. She started an after-school program to teach basic design principles, giving students a chance to explore their creativity and consider career options they had not imagined before. Her efforts inspired several students to pursue careers in creative fields, illustrating how sharing skills can change lives.

Exercise: Identify Skills to Share

List Your Skills: Write down your professional and personal skills.

Find Opportunities: Identify local centers, schools, or groups that could benefit from these skills.

Set Goals: Plan to volunteer a set number of hours each month or start a small skill-sharing group.

Reflective Question:
What skills could you offer to others, and how could they empower individuals or communities to reach new heights?

Acts of Kindness: Small Efforts, Big Impact

Small acts of kindness have a way of rippling outward, creating positivity, and building community. Research in positive psychology highlights that practicing kindness can increase happiness, lower stress, and promote a general sense of well-being (Lyubomirsky, Sheldon, & Schkade, 2005).

Everyday Acts of Kindness

Acts of kindness need not be grand gestures. They can be as simple as:

Offering a listening ear: Being fully present for a friend or colleague who needs to talk.

Volunteering time: Helping with local events or lending a hand to neighbors.

Expressing appreciation: Thanking people around us, from family members to coworkers, for their presence and support.

Case Study: The Power of a Smile

Jorge, a janitor at a large office building, made it a point to greet everyone with a warm smile. Over time, his cheerful attitude transformed the workplace, creating a friendly, welcoming atmosphere. Employees noticed that they felt happier and more connected simply from interacting with Jorge. His story shows that even the smallest acts of kindness can transform environments and elevate the spirits of those around us.

Exercise: Daily Kindness Challenge

Set an Intention: Each day, commit to performing at least one small act of kindness.

Reflect: At the end of the day, think about how it made you feel and how others reacted.

Record Your Actions: Keep a journal to note acts of kindness, promoting a habit of giving.

Reflective Question:
What small acts of kindness can you incorporate into your daily routine to uplift those around you?

Practicing Mindfulness in Action: Making Intentional Choices

Mindfulness, when applied to giving, enhances the quality of our contributions. When we give mindfully, we bring a greater awareness of our intentions and the impact of our actions. Research has shown that mindful giving enhances the joy and fulfillment of the giver, leading to more meaningful and effective contributions (Kabat-Zinn, 2003).

Case Study: Mindful Service in the Community

Tanya, a corporate lawyer, volunteered at a local soup kitchen once a month. Initially, she saw it as a task to be completed. But over time, she learned to interact more deeply with the people she served, listening to their stories. This mindful approach transformed her experience, creating a lasting impact on both her and the community members she served.

Exercise: Mindful Giving Practice

Pause and Reflect: Before each act of giving, pause to consider your intentions.

Observe Reactions: Notice how others respond and how it makes you feel.

Reflect on Impact: Afterward, reflect on the effect of your action on others and yourself.

Reflective Question:
How can mindfulness enhance the impact of your contributions, and what changes might you notice when you give mindfully?

Challenge yourself: What bold action can you take today to step beyond the ordinary?

Embracing Collaboration: Working Together for Greater Impact

Collaboration allows us to combine strengths and multiply the impact of our contributions. By partnering with others who share our passion, we can achieve goals that might be beyond our reach alone. Research on collective efficacy shows that individuals working together can create meaningful change by leveraging their combined resources, knowledge, and networks (Putnam, 2000).

Why Collaboration Is Powerful

Collaborative efforts bring diverse ideas, resources, and talents to the table, amplifying impact:

Diverse Perspectives: Collaboration brings together people from diverse backgrounds, enhancing creativity.

Increased Resources: Pooling resources allows for larger-scale efforts.

Strengthened Community Bonds: Working together promotes trust and unity.

Case Study: The Impact of Collective Action

Chris, a small business owner, partnered with other local shops to organize monthly street clean-up events. As more people joined, the initiative grew, transforming the neighborhood into a cleaner, more welcoming area. The success demonstrated how collaboration can achieve greater impact than isolated actions.

Exercise: Collaboration Challenge

Identify a Local Cause: Choose a cause that could benefit from a group effort.

Find Partners: Reach out to people or organizations that share your interest.

<u>Plan Together</u>: Brainstorm and strategize to create an effective action plan.

Reflective Question:
What projects or causes in your community could benefit from collaboration, and who could you partner with to amplify impact?

Legacy of Our Contributions: Inspiring Future Generations

Creating a lasting legacy requires a commitment to values and causes that extend beyond our lifetimes. When we contribute to meaningful causes, we leave behind a legacy that future generations can build upon. Research highlights that people who engage in socially responsible actions inspire others to follow, creating a ripple effect that benefits communities and society (Cohen & Janicki-Devers, 2012).

The Power of Giving

At its core, contribution is about giving from a place of love, compassion, and empathy. It is a recognition that we are all interconnected and that, by helping others, we uplift ourselves and our communities. When we focus on making a positive impact, we live in alignment with our higher purpose, gaining fulfillment that no material success can replace. This is what it means to live a life of significance.

As you move forward, consider how you can incorporate contribution into your life more intentionally. Reflect on the people, causes, and issues that matter to you and commit to making a difference in whatever way you can. Remember that every act, no matter how small, has the power to transform lives and build a legacy of kindness and impact.

How to Build a Legacy of Contribution

Inspire by Example: Demonstrate values through actions, setting a standard for those around you.

Commit to Causes You Believe In: Invest in causes that reflect your core values, building sustainable change.

Encourage Future Generations: Share stories and lessons with family or young people to pass on the importance of giving.

Reflective Exercise:
Write down the legacy you wish to leave. What causes or values would you like to inspire in others, and how can you begin creating this legacy today?

Embracing the Journey to Our Ideal Lives

As we reach the conclusion of our exploration into the foundational pillars of a fulfilled life, it is essential to recognize that these pillars do not exist in isolation. They are interconnected, each one strengthening the others in profound ways. Throughout this journey, we have delved into how personal development, health and well-being, relationships, career and purpose, financial stability, and contribution and impact come together to build a life filled with meaning and purpose. These elements do not merely enhance our personal lives; they create a ripple effect that extends into our families, communities, and the world at large.

A Commitment to Lifelong Growth

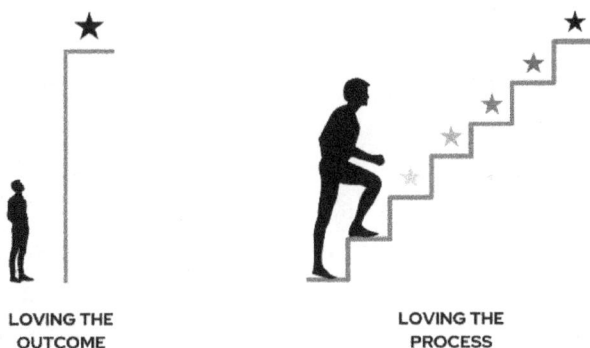

LOVING THE
OUTCOME

LOVING THE
PROCESS

Embracing this journey means accepting that growth is an evolving process, not a final destination. It is about consistently showing up for ourselves and those around us, understanding that each action taken today builds a better tomorrow. As we reflect on each pillar, let us delve into the impact they have on our lives and the lives of those we touch.

"When I look back on my journey, I see the struggles, the doubts, and the moments when I felt held back by my limitations. But each step, no matter how challenging, became a building block for a life that feels fulfilling and purposeful. The legacy you leave behind is not determined by your limitations but by how you choose to rise beyond them. Embrace the lessons, take pride in your progress, and know that every small step is a testament to your strength. This is your life, and you are more than capable of creating a legacy that inspires others to believe in themselves."

– E

Reflecting on Health and Well-Being

Our physical, mental, and emotional health is the cornerstone of a fulfilled life. Without a sturdy base of health, it becomes challenging to pursue other aspirations with vigor and determination. Numerous studies show that a balanced lifestyle, including regular exercise, adequate rest, and mindfulness practices, leads to higher levels of life satisfaction and productivity (Shanafelt & Noseworthy, 2017). By caring for our bodies and minds, we cultivate the energy and mental clarity needed to fully engage in life's opportunities.

Prioritizing Self-Care as a Form of Self-Respect

Self-care is often viewed as selfish, but it is, in fact, a profound act of self-respect and commitment. It allows us to maintain the inner resources required to serve others. Reflecting on my journey, I recall struggling to find balance after leaving the military. I had to relearn what self-care meant—recognizing that nurturing my mind and body was essential for my overall well-being. For those beginning their own journey, remember that self-care is not only about physical health; it is about creating a balanced, sustainable lifestyle that empowers you to show up fully in every area of life.

Reflective Question:
How do you prioritize your health and well-being? What small steps can you take daily to support a balanced life?

Challenge yourself: What bold action can you take today to step beyond the ordinary?

Aligning Career with Purpose

Our work shapes a sizable portion of our lives and can be a powerful avenue for fulfillment. Aligning career with purpose turns work into more than just a job; it becomes a source of satisfaction and meaning. Research consistently shows that people who feel a sense of purpose in their work report higher levels of engagement, resilience, and overall well-being (Dik et al., 2015).

Finding Purpose in Work

Aligning career with purpose involves seeking work that resonates with who we are and what we believe in. This often requires bold choices or even significant changes. After leaving the military, I sought work that reflected my values, leading me to the field of personal development. Helping others find fulfillment and meaning became my passion, transforming my career into a source of deep satisfaction. For those still on this journey, remember that it is never too late to pursue meaningful work. Whether it is through a career shift, a new project, or simply finding ways to add purpose to your current role, aligning your career with your values promotes a sense of purpose and enriches your life.

Reflective Exercise:
Identify what aspects of your current work align with your values. How could you bring more purpose into your professional life?

The Role of Financial Stability as a Foundation

Financial stability is the pillar that provides freedom and security, enabling us to pursue our passions and support those we love. Money itself is not the ultimate goal; it is a tool that allows us to focus on personal growth, meaningful work, and making an impact. Studies show that financial well-being is directly linked to mental health, life satisfaction, and personal stability (Dolan, Peasgood, & White, 2008).

Building Healthy Financial Habits

Jutta Heckhausen and Peter Gollwitzer's action phases model suggests that motivation is strongest when goals align with an individual's identity and values. Their research underscores the importance of pre-decisional planning to link personal meaning with actionable steps (Heckhausen & Gollwitzer, 1987).

Achieving financial stability involves adopting habits such as budgeting, saving, and mindful spending. It also requires learning to manage debt responsibly and building a foundation that can withstand unexpected challenges. Financial stability allowed me to invest in personal growth and pursue a path of service, freeing me from constant worry. As Benjamin Franklin said, "Beware of little expenses. A small leak will sink a great ship." Developing healthy financial habits creates a stable foundation, empowering you to live in alignment with your values.

Reflective Question:
What minor changes can you make today to strengthen your financial stability and support a life of freedom and purpose?

"As you reflect on this journey, remember that every challenge you've faced has brought you here, stronger and more resilient. The legacy you build is not defined by perfection but by your ability to rise above limitations and transform them into strengths. This is your story of resilience, a testament to your courage, growth, and commitment to a life of purpose. Embrace each step with gratitude and know that every small action contributes to a legacy that inspires others to rise as well."

-E

The Transformative Power of Contribution and Impact

One of the most rewarding aspects of a meaningful life is the positive impact we leave on others. Contribution and impact are at the heart of a life well-lived, promoting a sense of purpose and enhancing both physical and mental health (Lyubomirsky, Sheldon, & Schkade, 2005). By dedicating time, resources, and skills to benefit others, we create a ripple effect that extends beyond ourselves.

Small Acts with Big Effects

Contribution does not require grand gestures; it can be as simple as offering a helping hand, volunteering, or supporting a cause. Reflecting on my own life, I have seen how small acts of contribution have opened doors, strengthened relationships, and deepened my sense of purpose. As Helen Keller said, "Alone, we can do so little; together, we can do so much." I encourage you to explore ways to make a positive impact, recognizing that each act of kindness can uplift both you and those around you.

Reflective Exercise:
Identify one small act of kindness you can commit
to each week. Reflect on how this action impacts
both you and others.

The journey to fulfillment is not a straightforward
road; it is a dynamic, evolving process shaped by the
choices we make each day. The pillars serve as guiding
principles, helping us stay on track as we navigate the
challenges and opportunities of life.

-E

Embracing a Values-Driven Life

Living intentionally means making choices that align with our values and aspirations. This approach allows us to move through life with clarity and purpose. Here are some guiding principles to help you embrace a values-driven life:

Take Ownership

Embrace responsibility for your life and choices. Reflect on your values and set intentions that align with your vision. Regular reflection ensures your actions align with your highest aspirations.

Prioritize Growth

Growth is a lifelong journey. Embrace a growth mindset, seek learning opportunities, and celebrate milestones along the way. Every step forward, however small, brings you closer to your ideal self (Dweck, 2006).

Nurture Relationships

Invest time in building connections that inspire and uplift. Relationships based on trust, vulnerability, and empathy bring meaning and joy to our lives (Goleman, 1995).

Align Career with Purpose

Seek work that fuels your sense of purpose and remember that purpose-driven work benefits both you and those around you. A fulfilling career aligns with your core values.

Contribute to Positive Change

Look for opportunities to give back, whether through volunteering, mentoring, or supporting local causes. Contributions create a meaningful life and inspire others to join in making a positive difference.

Stepping into Your Ideal Life

Take a moment to reflect on the insights and lessons you have gathered along the way. Pursuing an ideal life is not about arriving at a final destination—it is a continuous, ever-evolving path. This journey offers limitless opportunities for growth, connection, and purpose, each step uniquely shaped by your individual experiences, values, and dreams.

Living intentionally and aligning with your true self requires consistent reflection, courage, and action. It is about embracing both the challenges and the victories as essential parts of the process. Every small step forward, each effort to live more authentically, brings you closer to a life that resonates deeply with your purpose.

Reflective Exercise:

Consider where you are now and where you want to go.

Ask yourself:

- What steps can I take today to move closer to my ideal self? Maybe it is setting a new goal, nurturing a relationship, or contributing to a cause that matters to you.

- How can I live in closer alignment with my values? Reflect on how minor changes in your daily choices can bring more purpose and meaning to your life.

- What will it mean to live with an open heart and commitment? Think about what it would feel like to approach each day with authenticity, courage, and a focus on growth.

These reflections are powerful tools. Embrace each step of this journey with an open heart and a steadfast commitment to your values and aspirations. Every action, no matter how small, contributes to a life filled with fulfillment and purpose. Remember to reflect on your progress, celebrate your achievements, and stay committed to realizing your highest potential.

Building a Legacy of Growth and Compassion

The quest for a meaningful life does not end with personal success; it extends to creating a legacy of growth, empathy, and inspiration. As you continue this journey, you are not only enhancing your own life but also positively influencing the lives of those around you. By living in alignment with your values, you become a source of inspiration, encouraging others to pursue their own paths to fulfillment.

Remember that your journey is unique, yet deeply interconnected with the lives of others. Each day presents new opportunities to gain experience, to be kind, to give back, and to inspire. This legacy of growth and compassion is the greatest gift you can give—not only to yourself but to the world around you.

Living with Purpose

Take a moment to envision your future. Mastering the 6 Pillars of Fulfillment Imagine, a life in which you fully embody your values, pursue your passions, and contribute to the greater good. Picture how your choices, actions, and relationships will evolve as you continue this journey. Know that the best is yet to come and that every step you take today builds toward a life rich with meaning and purpose.

Key Takeaways:

- Reflect on how this pillar aligns with your personal values.
- Identify one immediate step you can take to elevate your life in this area.
- Commit to acting today and tracking your progress.

Remember, every small step is a move toward the extraordinary. The time to act is now.

"You don't have to be great to start, but you have to start to be great."

— Zig Ziglar

7-Day Challenge Sheet

Each day of this challenge focuses on one of the six pillars, with the seventh day dedicated to reviewing and planning future growth.

Day 1

Personal Development – Embrace Growth

Challenge: Identify one area where you would like to elevate. Set a small, specific goal for this week that aligns with this area.

Action: Take one step toward that goal today, whether it is reading an article, writing a plan, or finding a course.

Reflection: How does working on this area make you feel about your potential? What do you hope to gain?

Day 2

Health and Well-Being – Fuel Your Energy

Challenge: Focus on enhancing your physical health today through exercise, nutrition, or rest.

Action: Plan and execute a healthy meal, a workout, or a relaxation routine. Consider what small, sustainable habits you could add to your routine.

Reflection: How did this action affect your energy and mood? What impact would making this a regular habit have on your life?

Day 3

Relationships – Strengthen Connections

Challenge: Strengthen one important relationship in your life.

Action: Reach out to a friend, family member, or partner and express your appreciation. Have a meaningful conversation or make plans together.

Reflection: How does this relationship support your well-being? What did you learn from the interaction?

Day 4

Career and Purpose – Align with Your Values

Challenge: Identify ways your career aligns (or could align) with your values and passions.

Action: Set one purpose-driven goal for your work that resonates with you. This could involve volunteering for a project, mentoring, or finding a new responsibility that energizes you.

Reflection: How does this goal give your work more meaning? What would you like to see change in your career over the next year?

Day 5

Financial Stability – Take Control of Your Finances

<u>Challenge:</u> Take a step toward improving your financial stability.

<u>Action</u>: Review your budget, identify unnecessary expenses, and set aside a small amount for savings or an emergency fund.

<u>Reflection</u>: How does financial clarity make you feel? What are your biggest financial priorities, and how can you make progress toward them?

Day 6

Contribution and Impact – Give Back

<u>Challenge</u>: Make a positive impact on someone or something today.

<u>Action</u>: Offer help, volunteer your time, or support a cause you care about. This could be a simple act of kindness, mentoring someone, or donating to a cause.

<u>Reflection</u>: How does contributing to others change your perspective? What kind of impact do you want to continue making?

Day 7

Review and Plan – Creating a Path Forward

Challenge: Reflect on the week and set intentions for continued growth in each pillar.

Action: Write down one achievable goal for each pillar that you will work on in the coming month.

Reflection: What were your biggest takeaways from this week? How do you envision your life changing as you keep working on these areas?

Reflective Exercises

These exercises invite readers to revisit each pillar and reflect on their journey toward fulfillment. Encourage readers to complete these reflections after the 7-day challenge or at the end of the book.

Personal Development Pillar Reflection

Question: What has been your most significant personal growth area, and how has it impacted your life?

Exercise: Write a letter to your future self, detailing the progress you have made and the growth you still want to see.

Health and Well-Being Pillar Reflection

Question: How has focusing on health elevated your daily life? What aspects of your health still need attention?

Exercise: Create a simple health plan outlining three specific actions you will take each week to elevate or maintain your physical and mental well-being.

Relationships Pillar Reflection

Question: What are the most meaningful relationships in your life, and how have they helped shape who you are?

Exercise: Write a brief note or message to one person who has supported your journey, expressing your gratitude.

Career and Purpose Pillar Reflection

Question: How aligned is your current career with your values? What would make it more fulfilling?

Exercise: List three professional goals for the next year, with actionable steps to make your work feel more purposeful.

Financial Stability Pillar Reflection

Question: How does financial stability impact your sense of security and happiness? What financial habits can you elevate?

Exercise: Write down your top financial goal and a plan to work towards it. Review your progress monthly.

Contribution and Impact Pillar Reflection

Question: How has giving back added meaning to your life? In what ways would you like to increase your impact?

Exercise: Identify one cause or community you would like to support in the next year. List three steps you can take to make a positive difference.

Final Reflection: Creating Your Vision

Question: How has your vision for a fulfilled life evolved through this journey? What legacy do you hope to create?

Exercise: Write a personal mission statement that reflects your commitment to these pillars. This mission statement serves as a reminder of the life you want to build and the actions you will take to sustain it.

Weekly Wellness Routine

Monday

Exercise Focus: Back and Biceps

EXERCISE	SETS X REPS
Deadlifts	4 x 8-10
Pull-Ups (Or Lat Pulldowns)	3 x 10-12
Bent Over Rows	3 x 10-12
Barbell Curls	3 x 10-12
Hammer Curls	3 x 10-12

"Build a strong foundation on Monday. Lift yourself to new heights, both physically and mentally."

Monday Grounding: Mental Health

Gratitude Journaling: Take a few minutes in the morning or before bed to write down three things for which you are grateful. This exercise can shift your focus towards positivity and enhance your mental well-being.

Mindfulness Meditation: Practice mindfulness for 10-15 minutes. Focus on your breath, observe your thoughts without judgment, and let go of stress. Regular mindfulness can reduce anxiety and elevate your mental clarity.

Call to Action:

Set Clear Goals: Define three specific goals for the week. These could be related to your personal development, career, or health. Setting clear objectives will give you a sense of direction and purpose.

Tuesday

Exercise Focus: Legs

EXERCISE	SETS X REPS
Squats	4 x 8-10
Lunges	3 x 10-12
Leg Press	3 x 10-12
Leg Curls	3 x 10-12
Calf Raises	4 x 10-15

"Tuesday is about leg strength. Your legs are your pillars of strength; strengthen them to stand taller."

Tuesday Grounding: Memory Retention

Brain Teasers and Puzzles: Challenge your brain with crossword puzzles, Sudoku, or brain teaser games. These activities stimulate cognitive function and memory retention.

Learn Something New: Dedicate time to learn a new skill, language, or instrument. Active learning helps create new neural pathways and elevates memory.

Call to Action:

Empower Others: Today, focus on uplifting others. Offer support, encouragement, or a helping hand to colleagues, friends, or family members. Helping others not only boosts their confidence but also strengthens their relationships.

Wednesday

Exercise Focus: Shoulders

EXERCISE	SETS X REPS
Military Press	4 x 8-10
Lateral Raises	3 x 10-12
Front Raises	3 x 10-12
Shrugs	4 x 10-12

"On Wednesday, shoulder the responsibility to rise above your limits. Your potential knows no bounds."

Wednesday Grounding: Productivity

Time Blocking: Plan your day by breaking it into time blocks dedicated to specific tasks. This method enhances focus, reduces procrastination, and increases productivity.

Set SMART Goals: Define Specific, Measurable, Achievable, Relevant, and Time-bound goals for the day. Setting clear objectives keeps you motivated and on track.

Call to Action:

Learn and Share: Dedicate time to learn something new and share it with someone. Whether it is a fascinating fact or a skill you acquired, sharing knowledge promotes connections and builds your own expertise.

Thursday

Exercise Focus: Arms

EXERCISE	SETS X REPS
Bench Press (For Triceps)	4 x 8-10
Skull Crushers	3 x 10-12
Barbell Curls (For Biceps)	4 x 10-12
Preacher Curls	3 x 10-12
Tricep Dips	3 x 10-12

"Thursday is about sculpting your arms. Your dedication will shape your success."

Thursday Grounding: Quality of Life

Physical Activity: Engage in regular exercise. Physical activity releases endorphins, reduces stress, and contributes to an overall better quality of life.

Spend Time in Nature: Take a walk in a park or spend time in nature. Connecting with the natural world can boost your mood, reduce anxiety, and elevate your quality of life.

Call to Action:

Express Gratitude: Reach out to someone you appreciate and express your gratitude. Let them know how much they mean to you. Gratitude deepens relationships and boosts your own sense of well-being.

Friday

<u>Exercise Focus</u>: Rest

"Rest is just as important as hard work. Allow your body to recover and prepare for the weekend ahead."

Stretching: Remember to breathe deeply and gently throughout the routine. Stretching should never be painful; it should provide a comfortable stretch. If you have any specific medical conditions or injuries, consult with a healthcare professional or physical therapist before starting a new stretching routine. Start daily stretching for elevated flexibility and relaxation!

<u>Friday Grounding</u>: Mental Health

<u>Positive Affirmations</u>: Create and repeat positive affirmations to boost self-esteem and promote a positive mindset. For example, "I am capable of achieving my goals."

<u>Connect with Loved Ones</u>: Spend time with friends or family or reach out to someone you care about. Social connections are essential for mental health and well-being.

Saturday

Exercise Focus: Legs

EXERCISE	SETS X REPS
Squats	4 x 8-10
Lunges	3 x 10-12
Leg Press	3 x 10-12
Leg Curls	3 x 10-12
Calf Raises	4 x 10-15

"Double down on leg day. Challenge yourself to go higher, one step at a time."

Saturday Focus: Memory Retention

Mnemonic Techniques: Use memory aids like acronyms, visualization, or storytelling to remember valuable information or lists more effectively.

Recall and Reflect: Take a moment to recall and reflect on the events of the week. Reflecting on your experiences enhances memory consolidation.

Call to Action:

Reflect and Plan: Reflect on your accomplishments throughout the week. Take note of your progress and plan your next steps. Self-reflection is a powerful tool for self-improvement.

Sunday

Exercise Focus: Chest and Triceps:

EXERCISE	SETS X REPS
Bench Press	4 x 8-10
Incline Bench Press	3 x 10-12
Dumbbell Flies	3 x 10-12
Push-Ups	3 x 10-12
Cable Crossovers	3 x 10-12

"Sunday, the day to expand your chest and your horizons. Reach for the stars, for the sky is not the limit."

Sunday Focus: Productivity

Weekly Planning: Set aside time to plan the upcoming week. Organize tasks, set priorities, and create a plan to boost your productivity and reduce stress.

Declutter and Simplify: Dedicate some time to declutter your physical and digital spaces. A clutter-free environment can help elevate focus and productivity.

Call to Action:

Connect with Loved Ones: Spend quality time with friends or family members. Strengthening bonds with loved ones enhances your emotional well-being and provides a support system to boost your confidence and trajectory.

References

Aknin, L., Dunn, E. W., & Norton, M. (2012). Prosocial behavior and well-being: A cross-national analysis. Journal of Happiness Studies, 13, 1–17.

Ariely, D. (2010). Predictably Irrational: The Hidden Forces That Shape Our Decisions. HarperCollins.

Bandura, A. (1977). Self-efficacy: Toward a unifying theory of behavioral change. Psychological Review, 84(2), 191–215.

Baumeister, R. F., & Leary, M. R. (1995). The need to belong: Desire for interpersonal attachments as a fundamental human motivation. Psychological Bulletin, 117(3), 497–529.

Blumenthal, J. A., et al. (1999). Effects of exercise training on older patients with major depression. Archives of Internal Medicine, 159, 2349–2356.

Bowlby, J. (1988). A Secure Base: Parent-Child Attachment and Healthy Human Development. Basic Books.

Brown, B. (2012). Daring Greatly: How the Courage to Be Vulnerable Transforms

The Way We Live, Love, Parent, and Lead. Gotham Books.

Cohen, S., & Janicki-Deverts, D. (2012). Social ties and health: An updated analysis. Psychological Science, 21(4), 534–539.

Cohen, S., & Wills, T. A. (1985). Stress, social support, and the buffering. hypothesis. Psychological Bulletin, 98(2), 310–357.

Cordain, L. (2011). The Paleo Answer: 7 Days to Lose Weight, Feel Great, Stay Young. Wiley.

Covey, S. R. (1989). The 7 Habits of Highly Effective People: Powerful Lessons in Personal Change. Simon & Schuster.

Deci, E. L., & Ryan, R. M. (two thousand). Self-determination theory and the facilitation of intrinsic motivation, social development, and well-being. American Psychologist, 55, 68–78.

Dolan, P., Peasgood, T., & White, M. (2008). Do we really know what makes us happy? A review of the economic literature on the factors associated with subjective well-being. Journal of Economic Psychology, 29, 94–122.

Dutton, J. E., & Heaphy, E. D. (2003). The power of high-quality connections at work. In Positive Organizational Scholarship: Foundations of a New Discipline (pp. 263–278).

Dweck, C. S. (2006). Mindset: The New

    Psychology of Success. Random House.

Emmons, R. A. (2016). The Little Book of

    Gratitude: Create a Life of Happiness

    and Well-being by Giving Thanks. Gaia.

Erickson, K. I., Hillman, C. H., & Kramer, A.

    F. (2011). Physical activity, brain,

    and cognition. Current Opinion in Behavioral
    Sciences, 2, 93–97.

Fredrickson, B. L. (2004). The broaden-and-

    build theory of positive emotions.

    Philosophical Transactions of the Royal Society of
    London, Series B, 359, 1367–1378.

Fredrickson, B. L. (2001). The role of positive

    emotions in positive psychology:

    The broaden-and-build theory of positive emotions.
    American Psychologist, 56(3), 218–226.

Garman, E. T., & Forgue, R. E. (2011).

    Personal Finance. Cengage Learning.

Goleman, D. (1995, 2006). Emotional

    Intelligence: Why It Can Matter More

    Than IQ. Bantam Books.

Gottman, J. M., & Silver, N. (2015). The Seven

    Principles for Making Marriage

    Work. Harmony Books.

Greenhaus, J. H., & Powell, G. N. (2006).

When work and family are allies: A

theory of work-family enrichment. Academy of Management Review, 31(1), 72–92.

Hall, D. T., & Chandler, D. E. (2005).

Psychological success: When the career is a

calling. Journal of Organizational Behavior, 26(2), 155–176.

Hillman, C. H., Erickson, K. I., & Kramer, A.

F. (2008). Be smart, exercise your

heart: Exercise effects on brain and cognition. Nature Reviews Neuroscience, 9, 58–65.

Judge, T. A., et al. (1998). The effects of work-

family conflict on job satisfaction

and life satisfaction. Journal of Applied Psychology, 83, 253–262.

Kabat-Zinn, J. (2003, 2015). Wherever You

Go, There You Are: Mindfulness

Meditation in Everyday Life. Hachette Books.

Kredlow, M. A., et al. (2015). The effects of

physical exercise on sleep and

emotional regulation: A review. Clinical Psychology Review, 34, 274–286.

Luthar, S. S., Cicchetti, D., & Becker, B. (two

thousand). The construct of resilience: A critical evaluation and guidelines for future work. Child Development, 71(3), 543–562.

Lyubomirsky, S., Sheldon, K. M., & Schkade,

D. (2005). Pursuing happiness: The

architecture of sustainable change. Review of General Psychology, 9, 111–131.

Maslach, C., & Leiter, M. P. (2016). The Truth About Burnout: How Organizations Cause Personal Stress and What to Do About It. Jossey-Bass.

Maslow, A. H. (1943). A theory of human motivation. Psychological Review, 50, 370–396.

Masten, A. S. (2001). Ordinary magic: Resilience processes in development. American Psychologist, 56(3), 227–238.

Peterson, M. D., et al. (2011). Resistance training for strength and longevity. Exercise and Sport Sciences Reviews, 39(2), 57–63.

Putnam, R. D. (two thousand). Bowling Alone: The Collapse and Revival of American Community. Simon & Schuster.

Rogers, C. R. (1961). On Becoming a Person: A Therapist's View of Psychotherapy. Houghton Mifflin.

Seligman, M. E. P. (2002). Authentic Happiness: Using the New Positive Psychology to Realize Your Potential for Lasting Fulfillment. Free Press.

About The Author:

Evan Pickett is an advocate for personal development, resilience, and holistic well-being. A veteran of the United States Army and alumni of Texas State University, Evan has dedicated his life to understanding and sharing the principles of growth and transformation. Having transitioned from military to civilian life, he faced and overcame significant challenges, including navigating the complexities of anxiety, dyslexia, and academic struggles. These experiences shaped his commitment to continuous learning and his belief in the power of perseverance and delayed gratification.

Evan is currently pursuing a master's degree, where he blends academic insights with his personal journey to explore the concept of becoming one's ideal self. Drawing from years of global travel and immersion in diverse cultures, he embraces adventure and the lessons it offers, promoting a deep appreciation for adaptability and growth.

Through his writing, Evan combines practical strategies, personal stories, and motivational insights, empowering readers to recognize their potential and create the life they truly desire. His book, Beyond Ordinary, distills these experiences into actionable steps, inspiring others to overcome their own challenges and embrace personal transformation.

Outside of his academic and writing pursuits, Evan enjoys spending time in nature, engaging with uplifting communities, and encouraging those around him to succeed. He believes that when individuals strive to become their best selves, they not only transform their own lives but also contribute to a brighter, more connected world.

www.ingramcontent.com/pod-product-compliance
Lightning Source LLC
LaVergne TN
LVHW011332080426
835513LV00006B/303